YOU TOO, PETER

PETER

15th Anniversary Edition

YOU TOO, PETER

15th Anniversary Edition

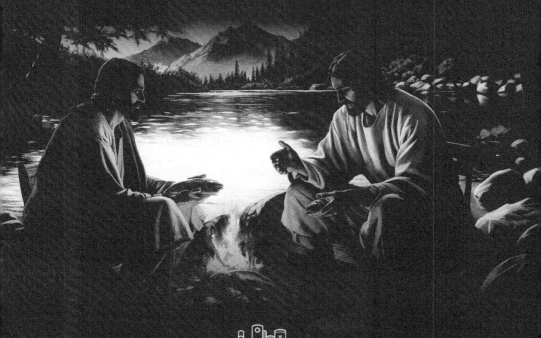

Davis Bookshelf

Galesburg, Illinois

You Too, Peter: 15th Anniversary Edition

Copyright 2009-2024 by Juanita E. Davis

First Edition: November 2024

All rights reserved solely by the author. The author guarantees all contents are original and do not infringe upon the legal rights of any other person or work. No part of this book may be reproduced in any form without the permission of the author. Scripture taken from the New King James Version Bible and the King James Version Bible. Copyright © 1982 by Thomas Nelson. Used by permission. All rights reserved.

Published by Davis Bookshelf
401 E. Main St., Ste. 163, Galesburg IL 61401
www.juanitaedavis.com
Tel. (309) 509-8881
E-mail: Info.davisbookshelf@gmail.com
Facebook: Davis Bookshelf LLC and Juanita E. Davis

Book cover design: elo_designs

ISBN: 979-8-9920044-0-3 (Paperback)

Printed in the United States of America

Dedication

This book is dedicated to my sons.

Acknowledgements

To God, our Father, and the Lord Jesus, in Whose 'blood we have redemption through, the forgiveness of sins, according to the riches of Your grace,' (Eph. 1:7). I thank You that You wanted me, called me unto Yourself, and that You are ever keeping me. I thank You that in July 1995, You reminded me that the meeting was still on!

To Randy, the man of my prayers. I am doubly blessed to have you in my life. I thank God for the gift that you are to me, your sons, the Church, and the Kingdom. I said it in the first edition of this book, and I still do: *You are one of the meekest, and therefore mightiest, of Kingdom warriors.*

To my wounded and hurting fellow disciples of Christ, He's waiting for you. The meeting is still on!

Foreword

Psalm 23 is as vivid a description of the Christian journey as could be penned at the leading of the Holy Spirit. The journey entails travel, forward progress, places of rest and a time of feast. It culminates with the promise of goodness and mercy following us all the days of our lives.

The only real hindrances to our advancement or forward progress in the Lord come in the form of hurt and offense. Along the Christian journey God designs and ordains stops and places of rest. Still waters, green pastures, and a feasting table represent times which facilitate forward advancement. We take unauthorized/unsanctioned stops and detours when we do not properly handle hurt and offense. They hinder progress and can become dangerous detours as well. If we do not learn to handle the hurt and offense that are sure to enter our lives, we will find ourselves stuck in a place of unprofitable times and fruitless endeavors.

Hurt and offense can most quickly develop into an endless maze or a downward spiral from which we have great difficulty freeing ourselves. For all of the discomfort and pain we endure, we have the greatest difficulty coming out of hurt and offense. If you fall into a cactus bed, it will inflict much pain. Staying still will only stop additional pain. Getting out of the cactus bed will require some new pain, but the effort and forward motion serve to eliminate the pain of being in the cactus bed altogether.

This book is sent by God to help those who may be trapped in the maze, on the slippery downward spiral, or are in the cactus bed of hurt and offense. As you read through the chapters, know that every word, syllable and letter are intended by God to put you back on the journey. The hurt and offense are simply steps on the way "through the valley of the shadow of death." Do not make the unauthorized and unsanctioned stop in hurt and offense. If you are there, be prepared to go through some more pain to get out.

I do not write these words simply because the author is my wife. God showed me as I read through the pages of this book that He seeks to heal a hurt and offended people through what He has spoken through my wife, the anointed author of this healing message from Him. If you are hurt or offended, allow the words of this book to walk you out of it. If you are not, then gift it to someone you know who is hurting or offended.

Pastor Randy H. Davis

Table of Contents

Introduction

You Too, Peter is a revision of A Message for for the Disciples...You Too, Peter, which I wrote and published in 2009. After publishing it, a well-meaning friend told me that I should not have added *disciples* to the title because a lot of Christians are not familiar with the term. What I discovered is that using it in the title served to be teachable moments, over the years. The only reason I omitted it from the title, fifteen years later, is for revision purposes; but, it is still undoubtedly a message for the disciples.

In Matthew 28:19, our Lord gave the commission to the disciples that were with Him then, and disciples today, to 'go therefore and make disciples of all nations.' When men are born again, although they automatically become children of God, they do not automatically become disciples (or followers) of Christ. That is why in Matthew 28:20, Jesus says, "...teaching them to all things that I have commanded you..." Men must be taught and disciplined to follow Christ. It is no different than when a baby is born. At birth, that child is not an automatic follower of good and right. That child has to be taught and made into a follower of good and right through observation of its parents or guardians, and others. I believe that if many Christians obeyed the command and commission of Matthew 28:18-20, in being disciple-makers, we would see less carnality and sin in our churches and in the lives of God's children – leaders and laity alike.

Just as I did in the first edition of this book, one thing that I will take care to explain is my distinction between the rest of the disciples and Peter. Many might ask, "Weren't all twelve of them disciples? They were. The distinction is not meant to imply that Peter was the

the greatest of all the disciples, or anything like it. In Mark 16, when the two Mary's (Mary Magdalene and Mary the mother of James), and Salome went to Jesus' tomb to anoint His body, they were met by an angel. After telling them that Jesus was no longer dead but risen, the angel then gave them a message for the disciples. In giving them the message, he did not just say, "Go and tell the disciples." No. He said for them to "go, tell His disciples *and Peter...*" Was it because Peter was so special? No.

It was because Peter had most likely written himself off from ever being used by Christ again, because of his denials of our Lord. Even after our risen Lord had appeared to Peter and the other disciples twice already. The third time was in Galilee (where they had been summoned for the meeting). The night before Jesus appeared to them for the third time, Peter declared to the other disciples that he was going fishing, which was his occupation when Jesus first called him to follow Him. The others' response to him was, "We are going with you also." (John 21:3)

That night, they fished to no avail. The next morning, Jesus appeared to them. The disciples did not know at first that it was Him. He asked them if they had a catch. When they told Him that they did not, our Lord told them to cast the net on the right side of the boat; and they caught an overwhelming amount of fish.

Upon hearing from John that it was Jesus Who stood before them, Peter arranged his garment, jumped out of the boat, and swam to the shore to meet Him. When Peter and the other disciples arrived at the shore, they found Jesus cooking fish over a fire. It was there during that seaside dining experience that Jesus – the Chef of chefs – not only prepared a meal of fish and bread for His disciples, but it is also where He restored and commissioned them all. *Peter too.*

From many accounts in the gospels, we can clearly see that Peter loved the Lord and had a deep-seated devotion to Him. However, just as his emotions drew him to the Lord, they also drew him away from Him – by way of his denials. As

Christ's disciples, we will all go through trials,tests, and temptations. Someone once said, "The greater the misery, the greater the ministry." That is the point that I am trying to make by making a distinction between Peter and the rest of the disciples. Peter had publicly vowed his devotion to our Lord. He also denied Him – not once but three times; only to have our Lord look directly at him, while he uttered his third denial. Can you imagine the degree of misery Peter must have felt in that moment, upon remembering Jesus' words?

In Luke 22, Jesus told His disciples one of them would betray Him. Then they began to ask among themselves who it was. They also began to argue about which one of them was the greatest. He then spoke to Peter: "Simon, Simon! Indeed, Satan has asked for you, that he may sift you as wheat. But I have prayed for you, that your faith should not fail; and when you have returned to Me, strengthen your brethren." (Luke 22:31-32)

The word for desired in the Greek is exaiteomai (pronounced ex-ahee-thé-om-ahee),

and it means "to demand (for trial)."[1]   Can we
conclude that in very much the same way that
Satan went before God's throne, and God
suggested Job to him (for trial) that Satan might
have gone to God and demanded (made
his desire known for) Peter – *for trial*?   Maybe
he thought that since God had suggested Job
that he would not wait for God to make a
suggestion, but would instead suggest his own
target to God by name. *Peter*. Peter's trial,
although not as lengthy nor physically,
financially, or socially incapacitating as
Job's could however be compared to Job's.
Although his was only a few days compared to
Job's, a safe guess would be that Peter's trial was
just as emotionally intense, or more. Why more?
Unlike Job, who did not heed his wife's advice
to curse God and die due to his offenses, Peter
denied our Lord due to offense.

Being that Peter was so
emotional, Satan counted on him to fall.
He wanted Peter out of the picture of his
own future — and ours. He hit him where

it hurt – and bad – in his relationship with his Lord. After denying Christ, Peter had to have been in a very deep pit of anguish, grief, guilt, remorse, and misery. *If not for that message though...*

Whoever you are, lay-member or leader, you may have purchased this book yourself, was gifted it, or checked it out at your local library. It might even be your hap that you have come across it on your desk or bookshelf (months, even years, after acquiring it). Whatever the case, there is a message in it for you – for today.

God wants to do something about the offense and the hurt that you are holding onto, or that you have imposed upon others. The offense and the hurt are not only affecting your relationships with others; but more importantly, it is affecting your relationship with God. He wants to change the way you deal with offense – making you unoffended, and eventually unoffendable. For every disciple of the Lord, offense is inevitable and necessary. However, the effects that it will have on us – if any at all – depends on each of us. Will we take it when it comes?

~~~~~~~~~~

Many times we deduce God to the Healer of only physical wounds and diseases, but I challenge you to think differently – God desires to heal the souls of men even more.

~~~~~~~~~~

~ Chapter One ~

Do Not Sorrow

*"Then he said to them, "Go your way, eat
the fat, drink the sweet, and send portions to
those for whom nothing is prepared; for this
day is holy to our Lord. Do not sorrow, for
the joy of the Lord is your strength."*
Nehemiah 88:10

It was in or around 444 B.C. that Nehemiah was
inspired to speak those words to God's people;
people who made the request of Ezra the priest that
he read to them from the Book of the Law. Seeing
their godly sorrow, while the law was being read,
Nehemiah encouraged the people with the
words that we read in verse 10. As Ezra read the

words of the Law, the people understood and received what was read to them. Then, in verse 9, we see where Nehemiah, along with Ezra and all of the Levites that taught the people, apparently witnessed the people mourning over what they were hearing. So, the leaders began to encourage the people, telling them not to mourn but to rejoice for it was the Lord's day. The key is that the people mourned over hearing the words of the law. But why? The law showed the people their sinfulness. As the words of the law (God's Word) were being read to the people, it was like a mirror was being held before them; and they could not deny what they were seeing. In the face of beauty (God's), they saw the ugliness of their own sinfulness.

The latter part of Nehemiah 8:10 is an oft-quoted verse of Scripture. I have even quoted it to encourage myself and others in times of discouragement. But for years, I did not know the actual reason why, nor the context in which, those words were first spoken. Hearing, "The joy of the Lord is your strength," should and does bring great comfort in discouraging times; but I cannot count one time that I personally quoted it to encourage myself or anyone else while mourning over my sinfulness or theirs. And though many along with me have borrowed from the context of that verse to encourage others, the proper context in which it was used – and should still primarily be used – has been seemingly lost; or, as was my case, not revealed due to lack of study.

In Matthew 5:44, Jesus says, "Blessed are those who mourn: for they shall be comforted." If you have done any study at all (whether light or intense) of Matthew 5, you would discover that Jesus' teachings on the Mount were about godly character in times of opposition (from others and from Satan by way of temptation) and that the mourning that He spoke of was mourning over sins first and foremost. After reading the *Sermon on the Mount*, if it were to be summed up with a question, the question would be, "How beautiful (inwardly) are you during times of opposition and persecution?" Sin uglies us, but mourning over it beautifies. In Nehemiah 8, at the reading, the hearing, and the understanding of the law, the people began to mourn – apparently over their own realized sinfulness and shortcomings. Witnessing this, the man of God (Nehemiah) comforted them with the following words: "Go your way, eat the fat, and drink the sweet, and send portions unto them for whom nothing is prepared: for this day is holy unto our Lord: *neither be ye sorry; for the joy of the Lord is your strength.*" (Italicized for emphasis)

"Neither be ye sorry..." The Hebrew word for that phrase is "átsab (*aw-tsab'*), and it means "to worry, pain, or anger...to worship, to wrest."[2] In other words, Nehemiah was saying to the people, "Neither worry, remain in pain, nor be angry, do not worship or wrest with the realization of your sinfulness nor the guilt of it." The Spirit of God inspired Nehemiah to speak the words that he spoke to the people, because God did not want the people to remain in the pit of sorrow. To ensure that they did not, God brought comfort in their mourning to end their mourning. Again, "Blessed are those who mourn, for they shall be comforted."

Since God did not want the people to remain

in the pit of sorrow, He encouraged them to get out of the pit by rejoicing in Him. The day that the words of the law were read to the people was actually the Feast of Trumpets. It was a holy day (a day set aside to God) and a day of rejoicing. God knew what day it was, and He knew that the people would mourn upon gaining understanding of the law and of realizing their own sinfulness. Just as He had purpose in showing them themselves through the Mirror of His Word,[3] He was also poised and ready to comfort them. And He did. I am sure that for the people what brought them comfort was to realize that even though they deserved death for their sins, God told them through His prophet to not remain in their sorrow but to rejoice. That's mercy, and it said a lot about their God to the people. It was not a day to look at self and assess all of its shortcomings and focus on them. It was instead a day to celebrate the Lord – and the people had all the more reason to.

In Psalm 118:24, the psalmist declared, "This is the day the Lord has made; We will rejoice and be glad in it." So, I say to the same to you. Every day is a day the Lord has made; therefore, every day is a day for rejoicing in Him. Just as God brought comfort to His people in 444 B.C., He wants to comfort you in your mourning. We are to mourn over sin (ours as well as others'), and we are blessed in doing so. However, our heavenly Father does not want us to become consumed with grief. How He combats that in our lives is to comfort us. The comfort that He brings to us is the knowledge that He is God Who loves us, and that He 'is faithful and just to forgive us and to cleanse us from all unrighteousness when we confess our sins to Him.'4 He is merciful in that He does not give us what our sins deserve – death without first giving us an opportunity to repent. He is gracious in that He has given us what we did not deserve because of our sins – salvation through His Son, Jesus Christ.

So, I say to you, "Do not sorrow [do not remain in your sorrow; do not worship your sins; do not worry over them; do not be angry]: forthe joy of the Lord is your strength [for gladness and rejoicing in the Lord are what will empower you to get out of the pit of despair and to stay out of it]." (Words in brackets mine). *Do not sorrow.*

To end this chapter, I will be careful to share this: The people that we read about in Nehemiah 8 humbled themselves before God. They submitted to Him. The words that Nehemiah spoke to them are not a blanket for all who sin. Sometimes there are people who hear the Word concerning sin and harden their hearts in pride.

God's message for them came through James, in James 4:1-10. Part of it reads: "Where do wars and fights come from among you? Do they not come from your desires for pleasure that war in your members?... But He gives more grace. Therefore, He says: "God resists the proud, But gives grace to the humble." Therefore submit to God. Resist the devil and he will flee from you. Draw near to God and He will draw near to you... Lament and mourn and weep! Let your laughter be turned to mourning and your joy to gloom. Humble yourselves in the sight of the Lord, and He will lift you up." One thing that we must remember about God is that as much as He is loving, merciful, and gracious, He is also just. Had the people in Nehemiah 8 not humbled themselves, God's judgment against them would have been James 4:1-10 – *before it was even penned.*

Questions

1. Have you ever mourned over your own sin? Explain.

2. Have you ever mourned over another Christian's sin(s)? Explain.

3. Have you ever mourned over the world's sin(s)? Explain.

4. With your own sin, was it easy to recover from your grief, or did you remain in a pit of misery and mourning—feeling as though God could no longer use you? Explain.

5. If you remained in a pit, what brought you out of it? Explain.

6. Are you still in the pit?

For your comfort:

"For all have sinned and fall short of the glory of God." Romans 3:23

My Story

In Nehemiah 8, the people requested that the Book of the Law be read to them by Ezra. I liken people attending a church service as doing the same. In essence, we are requesting that the Bible be read aloud to us by the pastor. As the Holy Spirit leads, the pastor reads and expounds on a portion of the Bible until we have understanding. As we know, the people in Nehemiah's day cried as a result of the conviction that they felt regarding their sin.

Once at a church service, I had a Nehemiah Eight experience. I usually sat near the front, but that day I happened to sit all the way in the very back due to something that was going on with my children. As the pastor read and expounded on the Scriptures, I was convicted and began to weep. I was convicted for my sin of holding a grudge and not having forgiven an offender, who had offended me. Just as He had convicted me though, the Holy Spirit also comforted me and restored joy to my penitent and broken heart.

As I was weeping, some of the people who saw me looked at me as if I was strange. Strange to me was that I was the only one weeping. *"For all the people wept..."* vs. 9

"The Lord is not slack concerning His promise, as some count slackness, but is longsuffering toward us, not willing that any should perish but that all should come to repentance."

2 Peter 3:9

~ Chapter Two ~

For the Joy of the Lord is Your Strength

"Then he said to them, "Go your way, eat the fat, drink the sweet, and send portions to those for whom nothing is prepared; for this day is holy to our Lord. Do not sorrow, for the joy of the Lord is your strength."
Nehemiah 8:10

In the previous chapter, we learned why Nehemiah said to the Israelites, "Do not sorrow, for the joy of the Lord is your strength" In this chapter, we are going to find out exactly what that joy and strength are. I will begin by telling you what joy is not. Joy is not based on anything external, such as happenings, things, and people. Happiness is events- and stuff-triggered, and can be feigned. Joy, on the other hand, is solely Christ-derived and cannot be feigned or faked. There is a song that I used to sing with my church's children's choir (the Sunbeam Choir) when I was a child. The song is *Jesus, You're the Center of My Joy*, and as I thought on the words of it just recently, I had an epiphany – an a-ha moment. Jesus truly is the center of our joy! That means that we can mourn over sin, the death of a loved one, or just be going through and still have joy. It means that if we keep Christ before us and our eyes on Him that we will not remain in the pit of discouragement and despair and be overcome with grief but will instead overcome grief through Christ. In our text, the Israelites were basically told to rejoice in the Lord, right after the wake-up call to their own sinfulness and shortcomings. They were literally commanded to go from the extreme of mourning to the extreme of being glad, with as much time to do it in as it took for them to hear it and to have it register in their minds. So, was Nehemiah being insensitive? No. Now that their eyes had been opened, the Lord desired that they focus on Him and not on themselves or their sins.

The Hebrew word for joy is chedvaâh (pronounced *khed-vaw'*),[5] which means "gladness". When one is told to rejoice, they are basically being told to joy again or to be glad again. Someone (even you), when realizing their sinfulness and shortcomings might say, "What do I have to be glad about? I am just a wretched and sinful person." Usually, the person will then go on to wrestle with guilt and anguish over their sins and over failing God. There would not be a whole lot, if anything, to be glad about, would there? That is where Jesus comes in. Think on Him, not you! Though we might feel quite unworthy, He is worthy! We are to take our eyes off of ourselves and our sinfulness and think on Him and His goodness and His faithfulness instead. We should think on His ability and His willingness to forgive us when we sin and ask for His forgiveness. We celebrate Him again... And again and again and again...! 'For the joy of the Lord [rejoicing in the Lord] is our strength.'

Strength? Strength for what? The Hebrew word for strength is mâ'ûz (pronounced *maw-ooz'*), which means "defense".[66] So, what Nehemiah was telling God's people was to not remain in their sorrow, and that what would empower them or make them strong enough to do so is rejoicing in the Lord. He was telling them to get their minds off of themselves, and to instead set their thoughts upon the Lord and His goodness. That is what would be their defense against remaining in the pit of sorrow or of even returning to it. At times when I have grieved over sins that I have committed, I found that the mourning can be like quicksand; and it can quickly suck you in. As you know, once a person begins to sink in quicksand, pulling them up out of it can be an almost impossible task. But, God! His joy has always been found to be strong enough to pull me up out of the muck and the mire of my pit of misery and despair. It is what gives all of us the fortitude to press past our own seemingly wretched selves and to make a press to the One Who is so very worthy of our rejoicing.

I have often heard it said at the news of some couples divorcing or a person committing suicide, "Oh, wow. They looked so happy when I last saw them," with *last* being a very recent time. One thing that we all must realize about happiness is that we can successfully put on our happy faces but feel miserable and near to death in the place that no one can see – *inside*. Joy, on the other hand, is something that originates from the inside and works its way out, no matter the state of our circumstances – good, bad, or indifferent. Why? Again, joy is Christ-derived. It is from and about the One Who never changes, but "is the same yesterday, and today, and forever."[7]

Romans 3:23 tells us that "all have sinned

and fall short of the glory of God." I hope that the knowledge of that is freeing for you. *All* means everyone – everyone except our Lord Jesus Christ that is. 'Though He was tempted in all points, He was without sin.'[8] He was tempted because He came to earth in a flesh suit, or body, with all of the same tendencies to sin that we have. The flesh was all new to Jesus, and Him being God *in the flesh* did not exempt Him from being tempted. In fact, by virtue of Him being in the flesh, He was a target for temptation. That is why because of having spent time in the flesh, He, the great High Priest, understands our weaknesses,[9] which is also why, instead of calling us trash and throwing us away when we sin, He bids us to "come boldly to the throne of grace, that we may obtain mercy and find grace [empowerment] to help in time of need [time of tempting]."[10] (Words in brackets mine)

We might feel like trash and so unworthy after we have sinned, and we might even treat others who have sinned like trash; but not our Lord. He does not operate like that. Instead, He invites us to come to Him, because it is He alone Who can wash away the stains from our sin-stained garments. Only he can neutralize the stink of our unrighteousness and cleanse us from it, causing us to once again smell like the perfume of Christ.[11]

Questions

1. Have you ever felt so full of joy after a "pit" experience that you thought you would burst if you tried to contain it? Please share.

2. How does being joyful feel? If you can, please explain.

3. Would you say that there is a distinct difference between being joyful and being happy? Why or why not?

4. In Psalm 51, a penitent King David, after sinning against the Lord, asked the Lord to renew the joy of His (God's) salvation unto him. Have you ever felt as though you needed a restoration of God's joy? Explain.

5. Do you still feel that way?

For your strengthening:

"The king shall have joy in Your strength, O Lord; And in Your salvation, how greatly shall he rejoice! Psalm 21:1

My Story

Seeing the people mourning, Nehemiah encouraged them to not mourn. He also encouraged them to have a party and not to be sorry, because the joy of the Lord was their strength. What?! Is it really that easy?

The passage from Nehemiah 8 should be one of the first that is taught to new believers. As a new believer, I would sin; and I would beat myself up for days afterwards. One time, after sinning (lying about something when confronted) I went into a deep depression (or pit) that lasted for months. It was a very dark time in my life. Looking back, I find it amazing how I had enough faith to believe in and receive Jesus, and God's forgiveness for my *sin* of unbelief in Jesus, but not enough to keep believing Him for forgiveness of my *sins* after receiving Him.

Like Peter, who returned to his occupation of fishing after denying Christ, I was contemplating returning to my old M.O. (modus operandi) because I felt that I would never get it right. What I realized was that I had to receive God's grace and trust Him to do the restorative, transforming work in me as I submitted to Him, daily.

"Whom having not seen you love. Though now you do not see Him, yet believing, you rejoice with joy inexpressible and full of glory."

1 Peter 1:8

~ Chapter Three ~

What's Your Flavor?

*"Who then is Paul, and who is Apollos, but
ministers through whom you believed, as the
Lord gave to each one? I planted, Apollos
watered, but God gave the increase.*
1 Corinthians 3:5-7

When I cook, I use very little seasonings. Although my family is used to foods being prepared that way, I realize that not everyone is. Therefore, when we have dinner guests, I will make seasonings available to them. My flavor preference is not bland. I just prefer the natural, unadulterated taste of the food. So, I make sure that when I do use seasonings that they will not take away from the natural flavor of the food, but will enhance it instead.

Sometimes when I am preparing meals, I think of the Church and its membership and attendance rates. It seems that today we have our own seasoning preferences for church, but especially for church leaders. Somehow some of us have adopted the mindset that we can have a flavor preference when it comes to choosing a pastor to follow and/or a church to attend. I have witnessed Christians – my fellow brothers- and sisters-in-Christ – not attend worship services simply because of who was or was not preaching on a particular Sunday morning or weekday night. The unadulterated Word of God (and mind you, it needs no enhancing) was still being preached in every instance, but the people stayed away because the speaker and/or his delivery style was not their flavor. Sad.

As sad as it is, my experiences were not the first time this type of mindset was witnessed; and it won't be the last. Paul addressed the Corinthian church in 2 Corinthians 3 for that very reason. At the time, many were boasting that they followed him, and others were boasting that they followed Apollos. In other words, the people had become groupies. Paul and Apollos were nothing but mere celebrities to them. What, or rather Whom, the people forgot was the one common denominator of the two leaders – God. Paul, in his letter, was reminding the Corinthian believers that he and Apollos – and any others, for that matter – could only do what they did because of God and by His grace. He also reminded them, or brought to their attention, that what was most important (the increase) came from God and not from any man.

Today, we have Christians who have left churches because a pastor of a race other than what the majority race was in the church was appointed to lead their congregation. Some have left churches because the pastor was not charismatic enough or was too much so. Some will drive or even fly for many miles just to attend churches that are led by well-known pastors, bypassing many local Bible-teaching, Truth-living churches on the way. Mind you, I do realize that some people are led by the Holy Spirit to make such sacrifices, but this message is for the ones who are not. This message is for the ones who only want to be attached to someone or something that makes them feel like Somebody and gives them bragging rights.

We have to be careful. A seed not watered will not flourish; and a seed over-watered will drown. In other words, we can link ourselves to whatever "Paul" or "Apollos" of our day, but if we are not abiding in (planted in) Christ, there will be no increase. There will be no fruit to display, because we will have only followed a man of God but not the Spirit of God. The fruit comes from Him. *"But the fruit of the Spirit is love, joy, peace, long-suffering, kindness, goodness, faithfulness, gentleness, self-control."*[12]

In verse 9 of our text, Paul went on to tell the Corinthians that he and Apollos are co-laborers. They were not striving or contending against one another but were actually contending together for the same cause – God's. It is sad to encounter

Christians who attend the church of a certain pastor, and they look down their noses at ones who do not follow that same leader. There is a word for that, and it is called prejudice. Then there are some Christians who will bad-mouth church leaders and denominations. Sometimes, unfortunately, they are only repeating what they have heard from the mouths of their pastors. It is time for us to wake up! God desires unity among the Body – His Body, the Church. Though there be many local churches, and many members, there is only one Body; and God wants us (His people) to be united in Him, not man.[13]

No matter what your flavor is – charisma or no; denominational or non; known leader or obscure – make sure that you go where you go because your spiritual flavor palate has been conditioned to God and His Word in that place. Make sure that you are where you are because you have tasted and seen that *God* is good[13] and you cannot seem to get enough of Him. Most importantly, make sure you acknowledged the Lord, and He directed your path to that place.

If you are where you are for any other reason, seek God. You might very well be where He has planted you, but are just in need of an attitude adjustment where man is concerned. Or you may have left or bypassed where you are ordained to be because it did not, or does not, suit your racial, emotional, denominational, or social taste.

In closing, I will leave you with the following: What if you had put all of your heart and soul into preparing a meal for someone or a number of people, only to have no one eat it? The food was good and good for them, but no one was interested in it. You later find out that they did not eat because you... Let's say because you served the food on paper plates rather than your fine china. Would you be offended? That's what we do to God's appointed and anointed leaders, but ultimately to God, when we refuse the message because of who it is being delivered through. God desires to get what is in His heart to our hearts by way of His menservants (to include women). But many times, we refuse what He has prepared – just for us – because of who it is delivered through or due to their delivery style. Many men and women of God have either been tempted to give up on ministry, or have just given up on it altogether, because of this. It is very offensive to know that you have labored before God on behalf of His people – people who will despise the very life-changing message that you have to deliver because you and/or your delivery style are simply...*not their flavor.*

If you are a leader who is tempted to give up due to that type of offense, please receive the message that is in this book. Always remember that it is truly not about you. When God's Word is rejected, He is rejected. When His messengers are rejected, He is rejected. If you are an offender, repent.

No longer miss the message because of who the messenger is or *is not.*

Questions

1. Have you ever not attended a worship service, not watched a Christian program, or disregarded a message because of who the messenger was or was not?

2. Do you have a racial, age, gender, denominational, or delivery style preference regarding who can give you a message from God?

3. Can you list some biblical examples of some of the most unlikely persons or things that God used as messengers in the Bible?

4. Have you ever been rejected or disrespected as a messenger of God? How did you feel?

5. Why do you attend the church that you do?

A little salt for you palate:

"Those who are planted in the house of the Lord shall flourish in the courts of our God. They shall still bear fruit in old age; They shall be fresh and flourishing."
Psalm 92:13-14

My Story

When we got married, church was easy for Randy and me. We attended a service at a military chapel regularly, sang on the choir, and served in ministry. What was *easy* about it was that we had no children at first. In the '90s, most military chapels offered no services for children, like nursery or children's church. So, once we began to have children, it became hard for me.

Sometimes I felt as though I left church services on Sunday's more discouraged than I had been when I went – simply because I was having to tend to one, and eventually two young children and still somehow manage to hear the preached Word. Although he felt my pain, Randy was not budging. He was convinced that the Lord had planted us in that particular church.

I too was convinced, but I began to get weary and discouraged. To be clear, I was not weary of being a mother – only of being a mother who *seemed* to be struggling alone. Our chaplain knew of my plight; and he, his wife, and Randy prayed with and encouraged me. Our prayers were heard. Eventually, God sent help, and I flourished greatly in that place.

"And a voice came to him, "Rise, Peter; kill and eat." But Peter said, "Not so, Lord! For I have never eaten anything common or unclean." And a voice spoke to him again and the second time, "What God has cleansed you must not call common." This was done three times.... While Peter thought about the vision, the Spirit said to him, "Behold, three men are seeking you... Then Peter opened his mouth and said: "In truth I perceive that God shows no partiality. But in every nation whoever fears Him and works righteousness is accepted by Him."

Acts 10:13-19

~ Chapter Four ~

So, Why Give Up On God?

*"Even today my complaint is bitter; my
hand is listless because of my groaning...
But He knows the way that I take; when He
has tested me, I shall come forth as gold.
My foot has held fast to His steps; I have
kept His way and not turned aside... I have
treasured the words of His mouth more
than my necessary food."* Job 12:2, 10-12

Have you ever had a bad restaurant experience?
I mean, the customer service was so terrible
that it just ruined what should have been a *fine
dining* experience, regardless to whether you were

eating at a fast-food restaurant or at a steakhouse. If you have ever had such an experience, what did you do to either resolve the issue or to at least make it known to management or even the owner? In most cases where customers have had bad dining experiences, they made the issue known to the restaurant manager who was on duty at the time. The manager, usually a neutral party, would then apologize to what seemed to be no end. Depending on the severity of the offense, he/she would then top off the verbal apology with a peace offering, which would usually be a free dessert,; the meal for the night being "on the house", or a gift certificate good for at least one free meal in the future. Most reputable restaurateurs will go to great lengths in order to ensure the happiness of their customers *and*…to keep them coming back.

Although it may happen, and very rarely I am sure, there are few people who would not accept the apology and the peace offering(s). Not only would most accept them, they would also not stop patronizing the restaurant. All parties involved would have agreed that an offense had gone forward, but they would have come to a peaceable agreement regarding it. In the probably very few cases where there was no resolution, the offended customer(s) would most likely stop patronizing the restaurant. They might even blacklist the restaurant in an effort to defame it. They would blacklist it by suggesting to others – verbally or by way of social media – to not eat at the restaurant. Never have I heard of anyone (and there may very well be people out there) that just stopped eating at restaurants altogether because they had a bad dining experience, outside of contracting a food-borne illness.

So, with all of that said, why are Christians so quick to not only stop going to church services but to also give up on God altogether due to a bad church experience? That is a question that my husband posed to a couple of our friends and me, one day in the summer of 2009. There are Christians who have blacklisted not just the Church but God as well after an offense. They become angry even at the mention of Jesus or/ God, and will try their best to undermine the credibility of the Word of God and the Person and Lordship of Jesus Christ – person-to-person as well as on social media.

Though people would rarely stop eating at restaurants altogether when offended, it is, however, very popular for them to stop attending church services and eating (reading, studying, and listening to) the Word of God because of a bad experience. They simply...*backslide*. During a great time of offense, and those from the mouths of his own close friends, Job said these words: "Even today my complaint is bitter; my hand is listless because of my groaning...But He knows the way that I take, and; when He has tested me, I shall come forth as gold. My foot has held fast to His steps; I have kept His way and not turned aside... I have treasured the words of His mouth more than my necessary food.."[15] Job could have been greatly offended, ultimately by God for not quickly vindicating him to his friends, and sunk into a pit of hopelessness and despair, but he did not – nor did he backslide. He knew that what would keep him during this time was the sustenance that he needed even more than his necessary, or natural, food – the Word of God.

A time of offense is no time to blacklist the church and/or church leaders. Most importantly, it is not a time to blacklist God. Just as it is not a time to blacklist, it is especially not a time to backslide. Like Job, it is a time for your feet to hold to the steps of our Lord, and to keep His way. He has ordained the steps of the righteous man.[16] What that means is that He has already walked the way that He desires for you to walk – and that is the way of Love. Though it may seem hard to cover over offenses with love,[17] it really does become easier knowing that Christ is not asking any of us to do what He has not. He is not asking any of us to walk in a way that He has not. He faced much persecution and offense during His time on earth as God incarnate (God in the flesh). But as He hung on the cross at Calvary, and I am sure that He was hurting intensely both physically and emotionally, He made a choice. He chose the way of Love. He rose above the physical pain and the emotional hurt (His character deeming that it be no other way), and He interceded for His offenders. "Father, forgive them; for they know not what they do."[18]

As I am writing this, there is a gospel song that has just come on the radio. I really had not listened to the message of the song until now, but how very timely and fitting it is for such a time as this! The message of the song encourages the listener to not give up on God because of His ability to fulfill His promises and His faithfulness to do so. If you have already given up on God (backslid) or are on the way to doing so, due to a church offense (or any other offense), don't. I challenge you to instead run to the Father by getting to know Him through reading, studying, hearing His Word preached, and praying to Him. Get to know our God and our Lord, and you will come to know that He is more than able to fight your battles and to defend you when offenses come (and they will). Because you know Him, **when** offenses come, you will be able to boldly take a stand and say, "That's not the Jesus that I know." Too often, we have deified Church leaders and other more (seemingly) mature Christians; but in the process have totally humanized Jesus. What that type of mindset causes us to do is to write Him off when offended by man (who is only a representative of Him), as though He is just another *mere man*.

As we mature in Christ and become more like Him, we will become more understanding and more forbearing – not excusing the offenses, but choosing to love and to intercede for our offenders in spite of the offenses. As we mature, we will find that we will also become less easily-offended as well. Sometimes we will even see that what we perceived to be an offense really was not. Years ago, one of my pastors taught about offense. What he was inspired to tell the hearers concerning offense was that one of the words that is used to define offense is "snare". As I have further studied the word and its definition, I have found that it also means "to entrap; to trip up; to entice to sin."[19]   So, I tell you offense is a trap. Do not fall for it. Do not go tripping over offenses. And do not let others get to you like that (enticing you to sin and), causing you to "lay down your salvation." Yes, offense hurts. No one is trying to downplay its effects, but the more Christlike and Christ-minded we become the more fortified and resilient we will become against it. Eventually, when it comes, we won't take it – only the lesson from it.

If you are ever offended by a fellow Christian, go to him/her concerning the matter. Christ has given us a prescribed way for handling offenses, and it is Matthew 18:15-17, "Moreover if your brother sins against you, go and tell him his fault between you and him alone. If he hears you, you have gained your brother. But if he will not hear, take with you one or two more, that 'by the mouth of two or three witnesses every word may be established.' And if he refuses to hear them, tell it to the church. But if he refuses even to hear the church, let him be to you like a heathen and a tax collector."[20]

In closing, when offended, let us look back at the example that was given in the beginning. All parties involved in the restaurant offense came to a peaceable agreement, and that was that an offense had taken place. The offended party did not give up on eating at that particular restaurant, or at restaurants period. The issue was resolved at the management (and lowest) level. However, in cases that cannot be resolved at the management level, the issue is taken from next-higher level to next-higher level (adding more people at each level) until there is a solution. *Hmmm?* I wonder where they adopted that principle from.

We Christians have the Spirit of Christ living in us. He did not give us a command and then leave us inept to do it. His Spirit equips and enables us to follow His prescription for resolving conflict and offense. With that said, why are we so much more apt to take the medicine that a doctor prescribes – and religiously – than we are to follow God's prescription? Don't get me wrong. We should take the medicine; but again, why are we so much more apt to follow man's prescriptions for healing in our bodies than we are to follow Jesus' prescribed way for healing in *His* Body? I will tell you why. It is because our very physical lives can depend on whether we take the medicine or not. That's why. Would it make a difference though if I told you that not only does your spiritual life depend on doing things the way that Christ has prescribed, but that your physical life *and* the spiritual lives of others do as well? The next time that a doctor writes out a prescription for you, try to read it. Illegible is what it will most likely be, and it will definitely be left up to someone else (a pharmacist most likely) to decipher it for you. God's prescription (His Word) for healthy living in every aspect is not illegible. It is clearly readable, and if you do not understand it, He will give you understanding.[21] So, I encourage you to read it.

I also greatly encourage you to not give up on God, because He is the One Who makes us able to love those who offend us and to confront them – *in love*. He is the One Who makes it possible for us to go to our heavenly Father and intercede on behalf of our offender(s), as He did in Luke 23 and as Job did in Job 42:8, 10. "But," You might argue, "my offender(s) knew what they were doing." Did they? How do know? Is it because of their title and/or position? Is it because they are/were your nearest and dearest friends? Lest you forget, dear one, it was not the church folk (the laity) who incited attacks against Christ the most. It was the leaders – the ones who taught the words of God's law to the people. They are the ones from whose mouths and hands was imputed the most offenses toward our Lord. It was not mere strangers who tried to convince Job that his afflictions were due to apparent sins, but his closest friends – the ones who knew him *friendtimately*. I implore you to follow in Christ's footsteps. Hold to His steps and keep His way. It will not exempt you from offense. In fact, it will most likely make you more prone to it. Never fear! He has led, and still leads, the way as your Shepherd. He will keep you. He will protect you. He is able, and He is willing!

The offering of peace that He has made to us all is Himself, for He is Jehovah-shalom – the Lord is Peace.

Questions

1. Have you (ever) stopped going to church, or given up on God, due to having been offended?

2. Who offended you?

3. What was the offense?

4. Did you try to blacklist the church? Did you try to encourage others to leave, or discourage others from attending?

5. Did you pray for your offender(s)?

6. Why or why not?

7. Did you confront your offender(s)?

8. Have you ever offended anyone?

For thus sayeth the Lord:

"Woe to the world because of offenses! For offenses must come, but woe to that man by whom the offense comes!"
Matthew 18:7

My Story

My husband has been a pastor for fourteen years. In that time, I have been offended more times than not. One of those times was when a member missed a Sunday service, because she felt that I had offended her. When I called her later in the week to check on her, she told me that she did not come to service the previous Sunday, because I had offended her. She dropped that bombshell on me, and it totally blindsided me. I asked her how had I offended her, she told me that I did not talk to her as much as I talked to other members. That hurt, because it was not true. I pointed out to her different examples of why it was not. Convinced, even though she did not apologize, she did agree with me that the offense was only perceived.

I told her if I had not called her, I may never have known I had "offended her." I also gave her Matthew 18:15 and told her not to give anyone (not me or anyone else) that much power that she would miss a service, or leave the church, over an offense. The next Sunday, she returned; and at first it was awkward between us. We got past it, and soon it was as if it had never happened.

*"Then Peter. turning around, saw the
disciple whom Jesus loved following, who
also had leaned on His breast at the
supper, and said, "Lord, who is the one
who betrays You?" Peter, seeing him,
said to Jesus, "But Lord, what about this
man?" Jesus said to him, "If I will that he
remain till I come, what is that to you?
You follow Me."*

John 21:20-22

~ Chapter Five ~

Hurting to Heal

*"For the Word of God is living and
powerful, and sharper than any two-edged
sword, piercing even to the division of soul
and spirit, and of joints and marrow, and is
a discerner of the thoughts and intents of
the heart."* Hebrews 4:12

As we continue our discussion on offense, let
me share this with you: People (even you)
may get offended by the hearing and the reading of
the Word of God. What the Word of God does is
offend the sinful nature that is in all of us – even
those of us who are born again. The sinful nature
(the "old man") will offend or it will be offended,

period. For all Christians, let us pray that if either has to be our position that it would only be the latter. The fact that the Word of God will offend is not just a supposition on my part. It is what it is, and it can be supported by Scripture; therefore, I will give you three supporting examples:

The first example is from a Book that we should be familiar with by now – the Book of Nehemiah. In Nehemiah 8:8, we read, "So they read *distinctly* from the book..." (Italics for emphasis) I looked up the Hebrew word and definition for distinctly, and I found that it is the word pârâsh (pronounced *paw-rash'*).[22] I was amazed to find that parts of the definition are *"to wound and to sting." Ouch.* It's no wonder the people wept and mourned at the reading of the words of the law. (Verse 9) How it must have wounded them and stung their consciences to realize just how sinful they were!

For further support, let's look at our second support Scripture – John, 6:61. In Chapter 6, we read where Jesus taught the Jews that He is the Bread of Life. While He was teaching, the Jews murmured at Jesus, but our Lord was not the least bit deterred or discouraged. He continued to teach them. The Jews' hearts were already hardened toward Christ, because He taught that He was the Messiah. Now, He's teaching them that He is the Bread of Life?! To say the least, like all of His other teachings, the Jews did not receive this one either. No surprise. Then in verse 61, we read that 'Jesus knew in Himself that the [twelve] disciples [also] complained at His teaching,' saying it was "a hard saying," vs. 60. (Words in brackets mine) Knowing this, our Lord asked them, "Does this offend you?"

Though the Hebrew word [skandalizō, pronounced *skan-dal-id'*-zo] for offend in this text is different than the one that I have recently discussed, the definition ("to entrap; to trip up; to entice to sin, apostasy, or displeasure; stumble)[23] is quite similar to it. In other words, our Lord was asking His the twelve disciples (His main followers), "Does this trip you up too?" Knowing that many other disciples would turn away from following Him because of that teaching, He was letting the twelve know that if *they* were tripping over the teaching about eating His flesh and drinking His blood, that they would also trip over future teachings – like what He would talk about in verse 62. *His Ascension.*

The third and last supporting Scripture that we will look at is Hebrews 4:12. "For the Word of God is living and powerful, and sharper than any two-edged sword, piercing even to the division of soul and spirit, and of joints and marrow, and is a discerner of the thoughts and intents of the heart." Imagine getting pierced by a one-edged sword, but a two-edged one! John Gill describes it as this: "It is "more cutting than one," by the words of His (the Lord's mouth), by the power of the Holy Spirit, and the efficacy of His grace; for His mouth itself is a sharp sword, and out of it comes forth one by which He pierces the hearts of men, cuts them to the quick, and lays them open."[24] *Ouch.*

Later, in another chapter of this book, you will come across a poem that I penned almost twenty-five years ago. It is titled *Who's Your God?*

The message that it had then is still a message for today. One of the stanzas in the poem reads, *"You won't read your Bible. Yet, for every conviction from the pulpit, you make the preacher liable..."* I reference that poem to make this point: If we would read the Word of God for ourselves, in our own private time, and stop relying solely on the preacher (who does indeed have his/her place in our lives) then we would not find ourselves "cut to the quick and laid open" in the public assembly for all to see. We would also not get mad at the preacher, holding him liable for the stinging Truth that is preached. God would also be able to do His work in us in our prayer closets, or rather *His* private Operating Room. Most often the messages that we hear over the pulpit would then be confirmation, and a bit more bearable, although just as convicting.

In the day of Nehemiah, the people (who asked Ezra to) had no choice but to have the words of the law read to them. The Holy Bible was not mass produced yet; therefore, they could not have their own personal copies to read in the confines of their own homes. In fact, the people could not have personal relationships with God—not like His we do today. The priests were the mediators between them and Him, and it was through the priests that the people heard from God – and it was usually in corporate settings such as the one in Nehemiah 8. What is our excuse today? Almost everyone has a Bible app on their phone, and we do not have to rely on anyone to read the Word of God to us. Also, we can have a personal relationship with the Father through Jesus. He is the Mediator between us and God.[25] When we believe on Him, the Son of God, we have immediate access to the Father through a Father-child relationship.

No matter how and where the cutting happens for you – whether in the privacy of your own space or in a corporate setting – thank God! Just as the wounding was for the good of the Israelites in Nehemiah 8, it is just as good for us today. Just as our Lord did not leave them for dead and forsake them, He will not do it to us. "...for he has said, I will never leave you, nor forsake you."[26] The Word of God tells us "a bruised reed He shall not break."[27] Our Lord will not bruise us to break us. A surgeon cuts a patient open in order to remove cancerous tissue or infected organs and then closes the patient back up. Is our God not much wiser and much more merciful and gracious than the one that He created that He also will not leave us open and bleeding out? Again, "Blessed are those that mourn [over sin – theirs and others'], for they shall be comforted."[28] (Words in brackets mine) The comfort that God brings is the sewing up of the incisions that His Word makes. It is the nursing of the wounds that His Word might impute. It is also the balm to the sting that His Word may bring.

God brings healing through His Word. It might hurt for a time, but healing will spring forth. During the hurting times, just remember that you are only hurting to heal and that, "For whom the Lord loves he chastens..."[29]

Questions

1. Have you ever been offended by the preached Word of God? Did you trip?

2. Have you ever said, "Ouch," in response to the preached Word?

3. Is God's Operating Room for you mostly private or public?

4. Do you know the difference between conviction and condemnation?

5. Why do you think the Israelites received what they heard with conviction?

6. Do you believe that the same message that is intended to offend the sinful nature can also heal the spirit and soul?

For your hurt and your healing?

"He will be as a sanctuary, But a stone of stumbling and a rock of offense to both the houses of Israel, As a trap and a snare to the inhabitants of Jerusalem."
Isaiah 8:14

My Story

Someone gave Pastor Randy a t-shirt that reads, "PASTOR WARNING: Anything You Say or Do Could Be Used in a Sermon." As many laughs as it gets, there are some people who won't find the message funny. I often say that most of us in the Church today could not have lived in Apostle Paul's day. He addressed the churches based on what he had witnessed himself or what was told to him by others – and at times, told who told him. God directs us to and plants His people in the churches that He knows will aid in our spiritual growth and soul development. So, pastors should boldly speak what the Holy Spirit gives them to say, and not fear hurting feelings.

There have been times during some of Randy's sermons, when all I could do was say, "Ouch." One time, it hurt so much that I told him it sounded like he was preaching directly at me. I knew that he had not been (not intentionally, anyway). What he preached was what the Holy Spirit had given him to speak. It hurt bad, but I grew from it.

Since I know that he speaks only as the Holy Spirit gives utterance, I have sat on the edge of my seat, for years of Sunday's, in anticipation of what *the Lord* has to say to me – even though it does not always feel good. *Ouch.*

"And when they [Peter and the other believers who were gathered with him] had prayed, the place where they were assembled together was shaken; and they were all filled with the Holy Spirit, and they spoke the Word of God with boldness." [Words in brackets mine for clarity]

Acts 4:31

~ Chapter Six ~

Offense is Not Partial

*"And when John had heard in prison the
works of Christ, he sent two of his disciples,
and said to Him, Are You the Coming One,
or do we look for another? Jesus answered
and said to them… And blessed is he who is
not offended because of Me."*
Matthew 11:2-4a and 66

Offense is not partial. It can happen to any of
us, no matter our position, title, or maturity
level. Just as offense is not partial to its *victims*, it is
also not partial as far as whom we are offended by.
Remember John the Baptist? John the Baptist who
was the forerunner for our Lord and Savior – the

one who preached in the wilderness of Judea saying, "Prepare the way of the Lord, make His paths straight."[30] This is the same John whom Jesus came to be baptized by, but forbidding Him, John asked Him, "I have need to be baptized of You, and are You coming to me?"[31] The same John who, while his mother Elizabeth was pregnant with him, leaped in her womb at the entrance of the one who was pregnant with the One Who was to come.[32] It was also this same John, who when imprisoned by King Herod for taking a stand for righteousness, *questioned the very identity of our Lord.*

Could it be that John became confused and overwhelmed by his imprisonment (his circumstances)? After all, he had just been out preaching Christ as the Messiah [mâshîyach (*maw-shee'-akh*) – "the One consecrated as King"][33] and preparing the way for Him. Now, he found himself imprisoned for reproving an adulterous king according to that same Standard (the Word) that he had preached about. Due to his circumstances, he was now questioning the identity of the One to Whom he had also not so long before deemed himself not worthy to baptize. John was offended, but not so much by his circumstances as he was by our Lord.

Offended, he sent that message to Jesus. John was no different from you and me whenever we get offended – especially after we have faithfully done what the Lord has commanded us to do. Our mindset becomes, "A favor-for-a-favor, a tit-for-a-tat." We want a bailout, and when our Lord does not come to our rescue fast enough (based on our clock), or even...*at all*, we begin to question His Lordship. In this case, I would assume that John was even questioning His Kingship. Just as John knew that the One Who was to come was also the Promised Messiah, *the One consecrated as King*, he also knew that He was the King of kings. With that knowledge, John knew that Jesus' authority surpassed that of any earthly king's, to include King Herod's. Knowing that, I am sure that he sat in that prison wondering, "So, why hasn't He come?!"

In answer to John's disciples and John's question of whether He was the One Who was to come or not, Jesus did not argue His identity and say, "I *Am* the One to come." Instead, He preached doctrines in John's disciples' hearing and performed miracles in their sight, then told them to go back and tell John what they had heard and seen. Think about it. I know that it took some time (days perhaps) for Jesus to teach John's disciples and to perform those miracles. Talk about adding fuel to the fire! With each passing day, John was probably becoming more and more offended. Then, instead of coming to bail him out, Jesus only sent a message to him. Part of that message being, "...blessed is he who is not offended by Me." In other words, the Lord said to John, "Fortunate; well off; happy is he, who is not enticed to sin or entrapped by how I do things." Jesus never bailed John out. We read later in Matthew 144 and Mark 6 that John was eventually beheaded by King Herod.

He was so offended by Jesus that after preaching Him as the One to come – the Messiah – he questioned His identity. He became offended by Him because he had faithfully said and done all that was commanded of him by Him – and look where it got him. *In jail.* You might be in a situation now, where you too are questioning the Lord. You have been faithful to Him – standing for righteousness in living according to His Word and by preaching it, teaching it, loving others, submitting to authority, praying and interceding for others... But now you find yourself in what seems to be a prison situation. Do not lose your head (no pun intended). Christ is your Head. Do not give up on Him. If you are not hearing from the Lord in the midst of your *prison experience*, then, 'Be still, and know that He is God; He will be exalted among the nations, He will be exalted in the earth!'[34] As you declared at your salvation, according to Romans 10:9-10, "Jesus *is* Lord!" I assure you that as Lord, He is just as able to keep you (while) in your prison situation as He is to bail you out of it.

Questions

1. Have you ever been offended by God because He did, or did not, do what you thought He should do?

2. Did you keep your Head (stay connected to Christ) about the situation, or did you desert or deny Him because of the offense?

3. Did you question Jesus' identity?

4. Are you currently in a *prison* situation?

5. If so, what is it? Health, relationship(s), money, church issues, etc.?

6. Are you wondering why Christ has not yet bailed you out?

7. Will you choose to trust in Him and no longer be offended by Him?

For your blessedness:

"...And they awoke Him and said to Him, "Teacher, do You not care that we are perishing?"" Mark 4:38b

My Story

Several years ago, my family went through a major financial crisis. After retiring from the military, my husband was blessed with a very well-paying job. He was also pastoring full-time at the church that we had planted, without pay. Things were going well for us, until they were not. My husband lost his job, after almost six and a half years. Although I had a photography business, it was not generating enough income to make up for what we had lost. It was devastating.

Like John, I had to be reminded that 'blessed are those who are not offended by Christ.' I wanted Jesus to come right away and make things "right" again – to bail us out of our situation soon. He did not. My husband and I were both faithfully serving the Lord, in life and in the church. However, unlike John, we still had much wisdom to gain. Through it all, we never stopped ministering and were reminded often of Hebrews 6:10. "For God is not unjust to forget your work and labor of love which you have shown toward His name, in that you have ministered to the saints, and do minister." As much as I thought we should close the church, sell our house, and pack up and move, *that* verse is what kept me grounded and unoffended.

"But may the God of all grace, Who called us to His eternal glory by Christ Jesus, after you have suffered a little while, perfect, establish, strengthen, and settle you. To Him be glory and the dominion forever and ever. Amen."

1 Peter 5:10-11

~ Chapter Seven ~

Familiar Territory

Read Judges 19:1-27

In the above passage of Scripture, we read the account of a Levite, whose concubine had played the harlot against him and then eventually left him – returning to her father's house. After some time, the Levite decided to go after his wife and show her kindness. Once he arrived at her father's house, the man stayed at his father-in-law's house for three days and then decided that it was time for him and his wife to return to their own home. At the news that they were about to leave, the father-in-law insisted that they stay another night. The man, having already been there f or three days, relented. So, for a total of five more days, he stayed yet "another night" at his father-in-law's insistence. Finally, on the afternoon of the fifth day, the man decided that it was indeed time to leave – despite his father-in-law's insistence that they remain another night. So, with concubine, servant, and asses in tow, the man set out that afternoon to return home.

The text tells us that they traveled until the day was "far spent." The travelers were probably tired and quite spent as well; so, upon arriving at Jebus (Jerusalem and the home of the Jebusites), the man's servant suggested to him that they lodge there for the night. But, being that Jebus was not a familiar territory (or home to his Israelite brothers), the man told his servant that they would not lodge there in a city of strangers. So, they pressed on for the familiar, and it was in Gibeah – a *familiar* and *friendly* territory – that they entered into, hoping to get lodging for the night. As was custom, the Levite and his travel companions entered into the city square and waited for someone to see their obvious need for lodging and to extend hospitality to them, but no one took them in. Finally, an old man came along, on his way home from work. Seeing their need, the old man offered them and their animals lodging for the night. The travelers accepted his offer.

After they were in the old man's house and were getting settled, some perverted men from the city surrounded the house and began beating on the door. They had no intention of going in and extending a neighborly welcome to the travelers. Instead, they were demanding that the old man send out the Levite so that they could have sex with him. The old man began to negotiate with them – his daughter and the Levite's concubine if they would just leave the Levite alone. The men would not agree to it, because they wanted the man. But since the men would not agree to the old man's terms, the Levite took it upon himself to preserve himself. He took his concubine and gave her to the men. Maybe they saw her and realized that she would do, because the text goes on to tell us that they took turns violating and abusing the woman all throughout the night. The next morning, after they were done with her, the woman went to the house where her husband was and fell down upon the doorstep. When her husband went to leave and go about his way (and apparently without his wife), he found her lying at the doorstep. Discovering her lying there, he simply said, "Get up and let us be going." His wife did not respond – neither by word nor by action. *She was dead.*

Close your mouth, dear one. What the men (to include her husband) did to that woman was no different than what some Christians do to their Christian brothers and sisters, in the name of hurt and offense. *Imagine*: A Christian brother gets caught up in a sin – playing the harlot to God. Another Christian (let's say, you) gently and calls him on his sin in hopes of restoring him back to God and to fellowship with the believers. But the brother turns on you and becomes verbally abusive and offensive. Eventually, because of his harlotry and unfaithfulness, he falls away from God and the Church and returns fully to the house of his previous father, Satan.

After a few months have passed, you decide to do the kindly thing and go after your lost brother, whom we will call *Lost-Again*. You go to the local bar where you have heard that he frequents each day after work. In an effort to get to him before he gets wasted, you arrive at the bar about thirty minutes before the time that you know he gets off work. You pegged it just right, because after about forty-five minutes, he comes in. He sees you right away, and although he looks quite stunned to see you, he comes over to the table where you are sitting. You motion for him to sit down, and he does. As soon as he sits down, *Lost-Again* begins to apologize to you for the mean and awful things that he said to you when you tried to restore him. You accept his apology and begin to speak kindly to him, hoping that this attempt at restoration will be successful. It is. After he tells you all of his deep, dark secrets and his reasons for falling away, *Lost-Again* assures you that he will return to the Church. Before the two of you part ways for the night, you pray with him.

That was a Friday night. On Saturday morning, you get a phone call. A Christian brother is having a get-together at his home, and he would like for you and your family to come. The only problem is that you had already accepted a dinner invitation from a non-Christian co-worker, for the same night. What do you do? Your wife believes that you all should go to the co-worker's function, since you had already committed to it. After reasoning within your mind and verbally juggling the two, "Non-Christian fellowship? Christian fellowship? Christian fellowship of course! "I would rather spend a Saturday night with *family* rather than strangers," you tell your wife. So, you call up the co-worker and tell him that you won't be able to attend his function. Rather than waiting for him to rejoin the Christian fellowship on Sunday, you then call up *Found-Again* (formerly known as *Lost-Again*) and ask him if he would like to go to the brother's function with you and your family. He accepts the invitation, and plans are set for that evening.

Saturday evening comes, and you and your family and *Found-Again* arrive at the brother's home. He greets you at the door and tells you to make yourselves at home. You get inside and see that you are the first guests to arrive, and you wonder among yourselves where everyone else is. Soon after you have gotten settled though, all the other twenty or so guests arrive together. Although many of the faces are somewhat familiar to you, you know none of the other guests personally. However, they are Christians, according to the host. About thirty minutes into the evening, one of the other guests suggests that the first party game be *Truth or Dare*. Most everyone (except you, your wife, the hosts, and *Found-Again*) agrees.

For some reason, it seems as though you are the primary target; and the questions that they ask are quite personal – questions that you feel could violate your wife's and your privacy. What do you do? In an effort to preserve yourself, you turn the attention to *Found-Again*. The host was not playing the game. He and his wife were busy serving the guests. If you turned the attention to your wife, your secrets were still at risk of being

being discovered. You know no one else. So, you put *Found-Again* out there. Until the game ended, he was the prime target. He could have gotten up and left, but he did not want to look like a wimp. So, he stayed and answered the questions, which were at most times deeply intimate and embarrassing. Sadly, you find that you almost liked him being put on the spot like that. After all, there was still the memory of him going off on you and verbally abusing you when you first attempted to restore him. The Levite probably felt much the same way in putting his concubine out there to be abused and violated by the perverse men. After all, she too had offended him by playing the harlot.

The night draws to a close, and it is quite late when you leave the get-together. You notice that *Found-Again* is quiet on the drive to his house, but you figure that he is just tired. When you arrive at his home, he quietly gets out of the car. In an effort to break the awkward silence, you cheerfully say "See you at church, tomorrow!"

No response.

In one night, your Christian brother has gone from *Lost-Again* to *Found-Again* to *Lost-Period*. You, ready to get about your way and on with another Sunday church service, fail to see that he was... *Spiritually dead*. Did I mention already that you are a leader in that church?

You later find out from your Christian brother, who hosted the get-together, that most of the guests that were at his house were people that attended the same church as he did – a church that he had only attended for two weeks. He did not know them that well when he invited them. Upon telling another church member about the event, the brother found out that the group was known for wanting to play *Truth or Dare* at functions such as what he had had. They loved to discover other people's secrets. They were also known to be the ones to steer clear of and to not talk to if you wanted your business to remain your business. Women and men alike, they were just a bunch of malicious gossips, not caring who they wounded or even murdered spiritually just for the sheer pleasure of discovering others' deepest secrets. You realize too late that you probably would have been better off taking your family and *Lost-Period* to the unsaved co-worker's function. As much as you recognized that it was your duty as your brother's keeper to protect him, you thought you were doing so by choosing to fellowship with other believers.

The scenario that I just painted might seem very unrealistic to you. No matter how unrealistic it may seem, just know that what is quite real is that there are Christian brothers and sisters falling away from God daily due to the effects of gossip and offense. Many are coming to the Church – us – wounded and dying; but we, ready to get about our way, are insensitively saying to them, "Get up..."

If you are reading this, who are you? The concubine? The Levite? One of the perverted men? Or the servant, whose advice was dismissed?

Questions

1. In the account in Judges 19:1-27, can you relate to any of the people? If yes, who?

2. Have you ever betrayed someone by gossiping about them?

3. If yes, how did it make you feel when you realized that you could have aided in their spiritual death due to gossip? Or did you?

4. Do you consider yourself to be safe territory?

5. Would others agree with you?

6. When needing a listening ear, do you wait for the leading of the Holy Spirit? Or do you call around and run to *familiar territory*?

7. Have you ever been betrayed by gossip?

For your vindication:

"No weapon formed against you shall prosper, and every tongue which rises against you in judgment you shall condemn."
Isaiah 54:17a

My Story

I once disobeyed the Lord by talking to someone in supposed confidence, after the Holy Spirit told me not to talk to that person about intimate issues anymore. The reason I talked to them was because they had called me and asked how I was doing, because I had "been on their mind." At the time, I was going through something; and I followed my emotions by talking to the person. She was familiar territory. She was also unsafe, because I later learned that she had betrayed my confidence to someone else.

The person that I realized that I was intended to talk to – God's choice – had called while I on the phone with the other person, but I did not take her call. Had I taken it, I could have avoided a lot of future heartache, but it was a lesson learned – and a valuable one. I realized that the person that I had considered to be a safe place, because I had talked to her before about other intimate issues, was no longer that. Sadly, I only realized it when I learned from someone else that she had told them my business.

I steered clear of her after that, and I repented to the Father for not waiting on Him. It was a lesson learned, and it caused me to strive even more to be a safe place for others.

"Men of Israel, hear these words: Jesus of Nazareth, a Man attested by God to you by miracles, wonders, and signs which God did through Him in your midst, as you yourselves also know – Him, being delivered by the determined purpose and foreknowledge of God, you have taken by lawless hands, have crucified, and put to death." (Peter)

Acts 2:22-23

Chapter Eight

That Ol' Crow, The Seedpicker

"Where no wood is, the fire goes out:
And where there is no talebearer, strife
ceases." Proverbs 26:20

If you are still reading this book after reading Chapter 7, good. Some people may question why such a vile act as gang rape was used in order to make a point about gossip and violating another's trust and privacy. The two are more parallel than we might think. Upon taking part in, and even leading, a women's Bible Study on the Book of Judges, I grieved as I read Judges 19. It was bad enough that from Chapter 1 of Judges, we witness a cycle of sin, and then them crying out to

God to deliver them. In chapters 7 and 21, we are told that the people had no king; and because of it, each did what seemed right to him.[35] My grief was not due to what happened in the Book of Judges as much as it was due to what is happening in the Church today. We have a God. We have a King, but some Christians live as though He does not exist, and they in turn do what seems right to them. Sexual perversion exists in the Church, but what is more prevalent than that but is just as damaging is gossip.

Gang rape – just rape, period – in the form of gossip happens every day in the Church. Church leaders join with their colleagues and disclose information that came to them when a couple that was on the verge of divorce sat in their office. The couple was holding onto hope that God would speak a healing word to them and that their marriage could be saved. Instead, their business was leaked, and they were laughed at. Church members join together for ladies' or men's nights out, and other church members become the topics of conversation. A lonely and desperate-for-friends woman joins with a clique or with another lonely woman, and they spend hours on the phone sharing – *their business as well as others'*. A church leader or member gets offended by someone else in the church and spills the beans. *Etcetera and etcetera.* The list of examples could go on and on, but in all or most examples that I have given or could give, the number one trigger (from the many others) for gossip boils down to this: *offense.* Having been on both sides of gossip, offense is the number one reason that people do it. Whenever someone offends us, we usually lose a certain amount of (if not all) respect for that person. It's easier to gossip about someone whom you do not respect than it is to gossip about someone whom you do. In the times that I have gossiped, I did it because someone offended me, or I was gossiped about because I offended someone. Never is it justifiable, because it is still an sin against God.

One thing that I will take care to point out is that (having been on both sides, laity and now leader) most Church leaders can be trusted to keep a confidence, and most nights out and woman-to-woman phone calls are wholesome and fruitful. So, don't be frightened away from those venues, but be discerning. Just as the Levite in Judges 19 should have listened to his servant for choosing a safe place to lodge, we are to use discernment and follow the Holy Spirit's leading as to what (or *who*) is a safe place or venue for us. As the Levite learned, familiar is not always friendly or safe.

In this chapter, we are going to look at two words and their definitions. The first word that we will discuss is rape. According to Merriam-Webster's Dictionary (MWD), rape means 1. a carrying away by force and 2. sexual intercourse by a man with a woman without her consent and chiefly by force or deception.[36] Looking at the definitions for rape, you might still be wondering how it has anything to do with gossip, right? Before I explain, let's look at one other word that is used to define rape – a word that MWD did not use in the actual definition of rape but did list as a synonym for it. That word is *violate*. It and gossip are interchangeable. Gossip, which is also known to be *a betrayal of trust*, violates a person's privacy as well as injures their ability to trust easily again – if at all.

"A carrying away by force" is the first definition that is given for rape, but what is being carried away by gossip? Can we assume that it is a person's rights to privacy and to first give consent for the matter to be discussed with others? The second definition is "sexual intercourse by a man with a woman without her consent and chiefly by force or deception". Whenever a person intentionally sets out to find out another's secrets, most of the time they are not going to just come out and ask for the information that they are seeking (although there are some who will). They especially will not demand that a person tells their business to them. Where physical rape occurs with more blatant force, mental; emotional; and informational rape (by way of gossip) occur more subtlety. A gossip will usually coerce information out of her victim by feigning concern or even by sharing, or trading, some of her own secrets. A gossip's main tactics for getting information are manipulation and deception. Intimidation is another tactic. Take *Lost-Period* in the previous chapter. He did not back out of the game of *Truth or Dare* because he was intimidated and did not want to look like a wimp. Some people will actually use their positions of power and authority to intimidate people into revealing their secrets.

When a person has been mentally and emotionally raped, their most intimate secrets have been carried away by force. When a person has been mentally and emotionally raped, they have consented to an intimate exchange of deep secrets. However, what they have not consented to was the retelling of them to others.

Now, let's look at *gossip* and its definitions. MWD defines gossip as a noun and as a verb, but we will only look at it as a noun. Later, we will study the Greek definition.

as well. MWD gives three definitions for gossip, and they are 1: a person who habitually reveals personal or sensational facts, 2: rumor or report of an intimate nature, and 3: an informal conversation. Looking at the first definition, we can see that the gossip reveals others' secrets for the sheer pleasure of it and possibly even for the drama that results from it – and he (yes, men gossip too) or she does it habitually. It somehow numbs the pain of their deeply-buried inner hurts and wounds. Although MWD defines the gossip as someone who does it habitually, be warned. All it takes for a bad habit to form is to do something just once and feel as though you have gotten away with it. Just because man may never find out, God sees and knows all; and gossip, like all sin, ultimately offends Him. Gossip, whether we know the Subject or not, is not right. Period. To learn what God thinks about it, here are some Bible verses about gossip: Leviticus 19:16; Proverbs 11:13, 20:19, 26:20, and 26:22.

Secondly, MWD tells us that gossip is a

rumor or report of an intimate nature. What more can I say?

Lastly, it says that it is an informal conversation. I like the use of the word informal. I like the use of it because some people really are more apt to tell their secrets (and others') in an informal setting – like when they are hanging out with the girls or the guys, are at home in their own space or are on the phone, etc. Don't believe me? Ask the many therapists and pastors who only get parts of the story from most of the people that they counsel – only to find out later that some key pieces were missing. Had the setting been less formal...

Now, we will look at the Greek definition of gossip. I saved it for last, since both the definition and the Greek word gave me a new perspective on the effects of gossip. I believe that it will do the same for you. The Greek word for gossip is spermologos [pronounced *sper-mol-og'-os*], which means "a seed picker (as the crow), that is (figuratively) a sponger, loafer (specifically a gossip or trifler in talk): - babbler"[37] Wow.

Before discovering that definition, I really did not have a clear perspective on the effects of gossip. Yes, I have been the *victim* of it, and I know all too well the deep hurt that goes along with knowing that someone played the role of a friend just to find out some of my secrets to either sell them for the friendship of another... Or to use them against me. I also know what it feels like to have betrayed another's confidence, even if they were considered to be a foe. I felt dirty. I did it because I was hurting. Hurting people are leaky, and that's why Christians especially are encouraged to be self-controlled and to talk to the Father about *every* thing. If there is someone that He can use to bring a healing word to us, then He will direct us to that person. That person will be mature enough to hear only what is necessary and to pray for us, and with us for our offender. Gossip is very damaging, because although it is sometimes true, it is also slanderous and defamatory (injuring a person and their reputation severely). Gossip can change the hearer's perception of others, plucking up any good ideas or thoughts that we may have had toward the subject. The main thing that gossip does is this (which is very, very dangerous): Gossip (or spermologos – sperm referring to seed; logos referring to the written Word) can pluck up the very seed of God's Word right from our hearts. Think about it: Your pastor has just preached another awesome and on-time message, and you know it is from God to you personally. Nobody can tell you nothin' 'bout your pastor. *He is a true man of God.* Then, during the week, the church gossip, who's never called before, calls under the guise of just calling to say, "Hello." The conversation is casual at first. Then she begins to talk about what is going on with the pastor. She tells of the pastor's alleged indiscretions; and she "knows it to be true because she witnessed some of it herself." You feel uncomfortable, but you listen anyway. You justify listening to it because you think you are mature enough to handle it. But, it proved to be too much for you. So now, instead of praying and interceding for him, you write him off; and take on the attitude of, "He can't tell me nothin' no more!" All, or at least most of, the Word God poured into you through your pastor has now been plucked up. That ol' crow – that seedpicker – was just used to not only discredit and defame your pastor but to also pluck up the seed of God's Word right from your heart, by way of your ear. Now you are lost, wondering, and wandering. Before, you were prospering (pushing forward) in life; but because the seed of God's Word that your pastor sowed has been plucked from your heart. A deposit of dung was left, and you now spurn the words that came, and now come, through your pastor.

What makes you listen to gossip about your pastor, other Church leaders, your fellow brothers- and sisters-in-Christ; and, yes, even the unsaved? I believe that that covers everyone. What makes you gossip? If you have found yourself in either position, think about it. What was the root issue? Most Church people gossip or entertain gossip about others because they have either been hurt and offended by those persons or by God because He is not using them as He is using those whom they are gossiping about. Now, out of frustration *and offense,* the gossips lash out at them, who in most cases are leaders. Miriam and Aaron could probably tell us all a thing or two about that, because they *went there* concerning Moses. (Read Numbers 1)

One other person who can tell us a thing or two about itt is Noah's son Ham. Genesis 9:20-27 gives us the account of Noah and how he drank wine from his vineyard, got drunk, and then lay in his tent naked. Upon seeing his nakedness, his son Ham went out and babbled about it to his two brothers, Shem and Japheth. Rather than joining in with him, the two took a blanket and backed into the tent (not wanting to see their father's shame) and covered him. When he woke up and realized what Ham had done, Noah cursed not Ham but his son Canaan. He blessed Shem and Japheth.

What Shem and Japheth did was honorable and showed a lot of maturity on each of their parts. They had heard enough about the their father from

Ham – enough to want to do something about it, and that was to cover their father's nakedness. How does that apply to us today? When *Ham* comes babbling to us about another's shame, we too should do the mature and honorable thing and cover them *in prayer*.

For years, decades, and centuries, gossip has been one of the main weapons used in the Church against laity and leaders alike. Before gaining the knowledge of the Hebrew definition for gossip (spermologos) I used to think of it only for the nasty spiritual dung deposits that it leaves. However, just as dangerous, if not more, is that gossip is a weapon of the devil that is used "to kill, steal, and destroy."[38] It can pluck up the very seed of the written Word that has been planted in our hearts. Crows are scavengers. They pluck up seed that has been planted, and they leave nasty deposits as well—*dung*. Let us squash gossip, let our lights so shine, and scare the crows away with the light of God upon us!

Questions

1. Have you ever been the "victim" of gossip?

2. Have you ever gossiped? How did you feel?

3. Before reading this book, did you realize just how damaging gossip can be?

4. Look up and write down Bible verses that talk about gossip, talebearing, and slander.

5. Is it too harsh to compare gossip to rape?

6. What will you do the next time that ol' crow, the seedpicker, tries to get in your ear?

For your own good as well as the Body's:

Gossip is like infection that leaks from an oozing wound – the hurting soul of the one who gossips. J.E. Davis

My Story

I once got offended by someone, whom prior to the offense, I had respected. They had offended me many times. One day, as I was talking about my offender to someone, it dawned on me that I no longer respected him. That lack of respect was why it was so easy for me to not only talk about what he had done to me, but also to reveal what I had heard that he had done to others. While talking, I realized I was gossiping and was deeply convicted. I apologized to the person that I was talking to. We both repented and prayed for the person.

I was convicted, and I felt dirty. I realized that my conversation about my offender was due to a lack and loss of respect for him and that I was causing someone else to also disrespect him. My offender was a church leader, who had already become noisy to me when he preached. By gossiping about him, I was causing someone else to also close their ears to him. I was doing just what a crow does. I was plucking up seed and leaving dung.

There is no offense or amount of respect lacking or lost for a person that justifies gossiping about them. If we talk about them, it should be only to pray *for* them.

"If you are reproached for the name of Christ, blessed are you, for the Spirit of glory and of God rests upon you. On their part, He is blasphemed, but on your part He is glorified. But let none of you suffer as a murderer, a thief, an evildoer, or as a busybody in other people's matters. Yet if anyone suffers as a Christian, let him not be ashamed, but let him glorify God in this matter."

1 Peter 4:14-16

~ Chapter Nine ~

Who's Your God?

"I am the Lord your God: Walk in My statutes, keep My judgments, and do them." Ezekiel 20:19

From the Fall of 2005 to the Spring of 2007, my family lived on a military base here in the United States. During that time, I found out that a family that lived near us were followers of a well-known Christian denomination that was prevalent in the part of the country where we lived. One day, I was in my front yard trimming my rose bushes, when I had the privilege (and it really proved to be that) of meeting the mother and her two younger children (of three). She was on her way from walking her school-aged child to the bus stop, which was only about twenty or so feet from my front doorstep.

That first meeting, we chatted and talked about rose bushes and the best time to trim them and other ways to maintain them. I had no idea that this one encounter would result in many unannounced, sporadic, and early-morning visits to my home. Her unannounced visits really bothered me at first. To add insult to injury, she would come into my house and boldly compare her home, her furniture, her husband (yep, her husband), and her children to mine. I soon overcame my irritation with her and just simply began to pray, "Lord, how would You have me minister to her?"

One day, shortly after I began to pray that prayer and after she had not come for awhile, I got a knock at my door. I was in the middle of studying a particular passage in the Bible when the knock came. Caught off guard, I laid down my open Bible and my notebook and went and answered the door. It was my neighbor and her two little ones. I greeted them and invited them in, and we went into my living room and sat down. There was no way that she could have missed my open Bible on the table. She let me know that she had not missed it, when while looking directly at it, she asked me, "So, what were you doing?"

I replied, "Studying a passage in the Bible."

She said, "I'm a Christian too." Then she named the denomination that she was part of.

Surprised that she said she was a Christian and a part of that particular denomination, I said, 'Oh. Is that a Christian denomination?'

She was full of surprises, because her reply was, "Oh, yeah. We're Christians too. The only difference between us and y'all other Christians is that we don't worship our pastors."

"Well, the nerve of her," I thought rather indignantly. I had not told her what denomination I was affiliated with (which at the time was non-denominational). Gathering myself, I replied, "We don't worship our pastors. But don't y'all have to read and live by not only the Holy Bible but also by a book that was written by the founder of your denomination?"

She was not the least bit surprised, nor thrown off by my question, and she showed it by answering with a rather proud affirmative. She then went on to further enlighten me about her denomination and about how she came to be a part of it. Her story was that from a young girl into her early teens, she went from foster home to foster home. Because she did, she experienced life and church in many Christian denominations. She told me that she had been baptized in water. She said that she spoke in tongues and that she was filled with the Holy Spirit. But *Who* she did not claim to know was the Father Himself. As she talked, I saw that like so many, she seemed to rely on every word from men's mouths and obviously did not read the Word for herself. Studying the Word, even after hearing a sermon, shows maturity, a desire to know Christ intimately, and nobility of character. (Ref. Acts 17:11) Realizing that she might not know the Lord, I graciously asked her, "Do you know Jesus Christ? Do you have a relationship with the heavenly Father?" She fumbled for an answer when she finally tried to give one, which was not as proudly or directly given as many of her other answers. In fact, she never said. To say the least, she also never knocked on my door again; not because of my question or any discomfort that it may have caused her though. I found out from another neighbor that her family had gotten short-notice military orders to move back to their home state. Upon hearing the news, I was actually sad; but, I thought, "Okay, Lord, You were teaching her something, weren't You?" How many of us know that the sandpaper effect is two-fold? As God was teaching her something, and she was rubbing me all the wrong way in the process, He was also teaching me something and smoothing me out as well.

After that last visit from my neighbor, I closed the door behind her and said, "Lord, I can't believe she said that Christians worship their pastors."

The nerve of her! What soon doused my little fire of indignation were the words spoken by the Holy Spirit. "You do."

*Okay, I have been surprised today. I have been not just dismayed, but **utterly** dismayed, and now this?!* I was shocked! I was also speechless, which was a good thing, because the Holy Spirit was able to continue speaking. "Worshiping them is not just in putting them on pedestals as if they could do no wrong. It's not just hanging on to every word from their mouths and not reading and studying My Word for yourselves to see if what they say is true. It's not just pursuing a relationship with them more than Me. It's not just serving them over Me. You also worship them when you deem them worthy enough to run you out of the places in which I have planted you." *An "ouch" went there.* You see, at that time I was struggling in the church – the God-appointed place – that I was in due to offense, and I had been all set to run away from it; at least up until that point anyway.

Wow. I was so enlightened that day…as well

as convicted. *Ouch.* Oh, I read and studied the Bible, and I checked for accuracy after each sermon or teaching at church or any other time I heard the Word preached. However, what leader had I deemed worthier than my God by staying out of (or even leaving) a place in which He had planted me? To worship something or someone means that you are placing so much worth in it/them that you live for it, it dictates your actions good or bad, and it takes up much of your conversation (you go on and on, speaking positively, *or even negatively*, about it). The realization that I had that day was grievous to say the least. I didn't just grieve over my own shortcomings, but for the Church at large as well. From that day forward, I became more keenly aware of the hero worship that goes on from my fellow saints for our leaders – our God-appointed leaders, who are put in place by Him but not to replace Him. All that hero worship for man produces is zero worship of the One Who is indeed truly worthy of all our praise, honor, and glory – *the Lord our God.*

Who's Your God?

The money ran out, today.
But whether you have it or not, I'm always
making a way out of no way. You have food,
clothing, shelter, and a bed in which to lay.
I have met all of your needs, and I even
awakened you to the dawning of another
day. Yet, not a "Thank You," have I heard
you say.

Who's your God?

You began to feel ill.
In a haste, you called the doctor first,
seeking healing only from a pill. My Son
was wounded that you may be healed,
and I created the doctor that he may be
*a **re**source, receiving his power from Me,*
***The** Source… Don't you know yet that I Am*
the Power to heal? Or maybe you deny the
Power that faith will reveal.

Who's your God?

You won't read your Bible.
Yet, for every conviction from the pulpit,
you make the preacher liable. I told him
to deliver My Word, that by you it may be
heard, hoping that one day you will begin to
search it and come to know Me for yourself,
that I may use you as an instrument – ever
so reliable. I need people who are willing to
arm themselves and serve – not be idle.

Who's your God?

Many Sunday mornings, you choose to skip
the fellowship. Instead, you stay under the
covers, snuggled with your
"significant other" – and throughout
the day, you satisfy your natural body
with what? Stuff like chips and dip?
The fellowship with other believers helps fill
your hungry and thirsty soul, encouraging
you, arming you – the sinful nature it helps

strip. And, One-on-one fellowship? You
slight Me, yet I am the One who knows the
number of hairs on your head, and each
passing day is like a pair of scissors going
snip, snip, snip,...

Who's your God?

Unrest comes upon you. And you run to the
phone, only to find that none of your friends
are home. Inside your head, Satan's lies
continue to roam because you continue to
bypass My throne. Seek My face that I may
give you peace and reassure you of Whose
you are – descendant of Abraham, My heir,
Christ's co-heir, a victor not a victim
– submit to Me, resist the devil, and he will
flee. Come to Me! Come, I bid you. Yet,
aimlessly and blindly you continue to roam,
refusing to wash in the "pool of Siloam".[39]

Who's your God?

*Early in the morning, while it is still dark,
My Spirit awakens you to pray. "But it's
too early in the morning. It's still dark out.
I'm so tired. I have a long day," you say.
And there you continue to lay. Don't you
know that it could have been My plan that
you not even see the dawning of this day?*

Who's your God?

*In church, I want you to give Me praise, but
you look around at your neighbors, and not
a hand or a "Thank You, Lord!" you will
raise. Man is not your Creator, I am! For
him you will labor, but before him, for Me,
you won't? Don't you know that in times of
trouble, he will leave you; but I will remain
with you for all of your days? Yet your
excuse remains, "I don't have to be loud or
lift my hands. It doesn't take all that.
Besides, God knows my heart." That's right,
I do; and just a little bit of praise might
allow Me to navigate the maze.*

Who's your God?

Over and over, My Son has stood knocking at the door of your hardened heart, but of that "Jesus thing" you said you want no part. In making that decision, you thought you were being smart. But don't you know yet that to get to Me, He is the Way – and not by your own effort or any other's? **Only** *through Him can a journey, a Father-child relationship, with Me ever start.*

Who's your God?

Copyright 2001-2009, 2024 © Juanita E. Davis

Questions

1. Who's your God?

2. To whom do you give the most words, thoughts, and attention to?

3. Have you ever left a church, a job, or elsewhere (knowing that God had planted you there) because of an offender?

4. If yes, what were the circumstances under which you left?

5. Looking back on it, was your leaving emotion-driven or Spirit-led?

6. Obedience is an act of worship. If the Lord tells you to stay in a hard place, would you?

7. What does Matthew 10:14 mean to you?

8. Who's your God?

For your comfort:

"Then was Jesus led up of the Spirit into the wilderness to be tempted of the devil."
Matthew 4:1-11

My Story

Over the years, I have thought about my neighbor often and wondered where she and her family are. I have especially wondered if she has come to know Christ (more). I have also hoped that despite my inwardly bad attitude at first – of feeling inconvenienced and of judging her and those in her denomination – that there was *something* that I said or did over time (and even that first day) that allowed her to see Jesus more clearly. Her words and actions most definitely made me see Him from a broader perspective.

She never answered my question of whether she knew Jesus. Looking back, just her telling me that she was a Christian should have been enough for me. Her accountability was to God, not me. Whether she was or not was between her and Him. I judged her and questioned her salvation based on a stereotype of the denomination she was affiliated with. She judged me based on my not being affiliated with her denomination.

My encounter with her that first time was an encounter with Christ. Of all the questions that she and I asked one another, He was asking at least me, *"Who's your God?"*

"You therefore, beloved, since you know this beforehand, beware lest you also fall from your own steadfastness, being led away with the error of the wicked; but grow in the grace and knowledge of our Lord and Savior Jesus Christ. To Him be glory both now and forever. Amen."

2 Peter 3:17-18

~ *Chapter Ten* ~

Who Do Men Say He Is?

"When Jesus came into the region of Caesarea Philippi, He asked His disciples, saying, "Who do men say that I, the Son of Man, am?" Matthew 16:13

One thing that has seemed to always succeed in putting a bad taste in some Christians' mouths is for them to watch a secular awards show (or to see a news clip of one) and hear a raunchy-acting (and most likely, riotous-living) and/or scantily-clad award recipient thank God for their success.

"God is good! I wanna thank Him..." Why would it give anyone a bad taste? What they have just stood before most of North America (possibly most of the world) and done was actually in keeping with the Word of God. Psalm 150:66 says, "Let everything that has breath praise the Lord. Praise the Lord!" God is due the thanksgiving and the praise, because He is the One who gave them the gift to do what it is that they were awarded for. Keep reading.

I have heard many an interview where a secular artist was being interviewed. Upon being asked where they got their start, the answer has, a huge percentage of the time, been, "In the Church." So, because they got their start in the Church, they were well aware of the Church lingo. They knew what men said about Christ, and they also knew Whom men (Grandma, Grandpa, Mom, Dad, Auntie, Pastor So-and-So, etc.) said that He is. So, when they were awarded and recognized for the

the talents and gifts, they thanked God and said of Him what they had heard other men say.

Instead of using the gifts that they were praising God for *for* His glory, what they did with them and the grace afforded them by Him was got them and went off into a far country (the world). They got the goods, went away from God, and began to live as prodigals (MWD: someone who is "recklessly extravagant: LUXURIANT: wasteful: lavish" in their living).[40]

This story sounds familiar, doesn't it? You did not think that a book that is to be used as a tool for restoring backsliders back to God would be void of the *Story of the Prodigal Son*, did you? We read in Luke 15:11-32 that the younger son of two asked his father for his inheritance, *prior to* his father's death. The father obliged, and the son took it and went away to a far off country, where he lived riotously. His inheritance and all that he had soon ran out, and then a famine hit the land. The son had nothing, and because he had nothing he went to a citizen of the country, who tasked him to feed his swine. The son, having no food to eat nor any means to buy any, became so hungry that he would have eaten the husks that were fed to the pigs – only no one gave him any. That woke him up! He then recounted how his father's hired servants had more than enough to eat; so, he decided that he would return to his father, repent, and offer to become one of his hired servants. We then read that he returned to his father,; and his father seeing him from afar off, ran to him and kissed him. The son repented and began his offer to his father, as he had contemplated, but his father would not hear it and instead gave him a grand reception as his once-dead son.

The text tells us that the son *came to himself* (Luke 15:17), or he came to his senses as some versions of the Bible read. Take note, immediately after coming to himself, the son remembered one person – *his father*. Yes, he realized his state compared to that of his father's hired servants, but the state of the hired servants was due to the character of their master, his father. The son had lived in the father's house. He had been in his father's presence. He had communed with him daily, and He knew his father. So, although the realization that he had, soon after coming to himself, was about the state of his father's hired servants versus his present state, the remembrance that he had is what is so much more profound and key to the text. He *remembered* his father – and not only did he remember his father, he remembered his father's attributes as well as his character. He knew that all he had to do was return to his father, and his father would receive him back – *even if it was in the position of servant.*

I believe that there are many – whether it be singers, actors, businessmen/women, co-workers, our neighbors – who have gotten their inheritance (the gifts and the grace) from God and then left Him to go away to the far off country of the world. They got their start in the Church, but soon church was unappealing to them. They got hurt in church. They saw the Church as a beggar. There were few opportunities to be financially wealthy in the Church. The list could go on and on. Now, they might go to church several times a year as a favor to Mom and Dad or Grandma and Grandpa – or even God. They might go to church, because it is simply the *right thing to do*. Another way that they might get *their time in* or *serve* God is to donate money or other resources to the Church or record a gospel song (or even an entire album). All while continuing to live as prodigals. Their hearts are still in the far off country – but they are *serving* God, right?

In Luke 15:11-32, the prodigal son physically returned to his earthly father. Today, we can go through the physical motions of attending church, giving to churches and charities, and…praising the Lord when we are awarded and recognized for our achievements. But we can do that and have hearts that are far from Him. Going back to the beginning of this chapter, many will praise the Lord, attributing their success to Him, but do not be fooled. Though you are right in praising Him for the gift(s) and the ability to do what you do, it is wrong to believe that He has ordained you to be where you are – living as a prodigal and displaying little to no morals. Some, who live lives far from the Father will even say publicly how blessed they are. Understand this, having the blessing of the Father is having Him speak well of you – because you are living *in accordance* with His Standard. Too many times, we expect God to bow down to our standards, rather than us rising up to His Standard, Who is the Son of God, Jesus Christ, the epitome of righteousness.

Consider this example: You are working on a project – say you are building a dollhouse. You go to the hardware store and have all the wood cut to the specs that you need, and you return home to get started on your project. At some point you realize that one of the pieces of wood, which has to be twelve inches long, is only eleven and three quarters of an inch long. What do you do? Do you cut down the foot-long ruler in order for it to measure up to the piece of wood? No! You either add to the piece of wood until it measures *up to* twelve inches, or you go back to the hardware store and have them cut the correct size for you. To cut down the ruler, which is the Universal Standard of Measurement, to comply with the piece of wood that does not measure up is ridiculous. It is even more ridiculous for us to expect God, *the Ruler*, to bow down to our standards (our compromised way of living) and then call us blessed. He has set the Standard before us, and that Standard is Christ the Lord.

If Christ was to ask many professed Christians, as He asked His disciples in Matthew 16, "But whom do men say that I am," most (like His disciples then) would probably have a ready answer, with what others have said about Him. Today, many profess to be Christians, but many are not following Christ at all. They are not true disciples. We must do a personal assessment of ourselves and of our profession of being Christians. Jesus is the only way to the Father. He is the Way.[41] Some believe that they are Christians because they were raised in church. Going to church, and even spending every Sunday of your life there, does not make one a Christian. The fact that our parents, grandparents, or those who raised us are/were Christians also does not make us Christians. We are not born naturally into Christianity; but are rather re-born spiritually into it. We cannot ride through life, and especially to heaven, on someone else's coattails of faith in, or their profession of, faith. Many have tried it, and that is why many have fallen away so easily – and still are. We must know Christ/for ourselves.

Coming to himself, the "prodigal son" remembered his father and the *kind of* father he was. He knew his father well enough to know that if he just returned to him that his father would receive him back, even as a hired servant. Maybe you too have come to yourself. Sure, you have plenty of food and means to buy more, but you have become tired of living in a far off country that has nothing good to offer your soul – only what's fit for swine. You have become tired of living among and smelling like swine, but you are at a standstill. You stay where you are because you only know of the Father through hearsay, and you are not sure that that He would receive you back – not even as a servant. To test the waters though, you choose to serve Him on your terms by doing good deeds for the Church – with your hire being the gifts you give and the things you do. The father of the prodigal son would not receive him back as just a "hired" servant, and God won't settle either. In John 15:15, Jesus says, "No longer do I call you servants... but I have called you friends..." God won't settle; so, why would you? He will receive you. The Father is waiting to receive you back as His once-dead-in-sin child. He's waiting....

Questions

1. What comes to mind when you hear unsaved people praising the Lord?

2. Did you praise Him when you were unsaved?

3. Can you relate to the prodigal son?

4. If so, what experience brought you to the end of yourself?

5. If Christ was to ask you, "Whom do men say that I am," what would you say?

6. Do you know God as Father?

7. Look up and list Bible verses that talk about God as Father.

For His exaltation:

"Let every thing that hath breath praise the LORD. Praise ye the LORD." Psalm 150:6

My Story

Earlier on in my walk with the Lord, it used to bother me when I would hear ungodly people say how they owed their success or an award to God. It bothered me because it was evident that those people were not living for Christ, and I felt as though they were giving the impression to others that God was okay with their lifestyles. Then one day, I was enlightened by Psalm 150:6, which says, "Let everything that has breath praise the Lord." That word *everything* leaves nothing and no one out, and it also leaves no room for excuses for anyone or anything to not praise the Lord. Those once-bothersome people whose lives showed no evidence that they believed God, but whose praise of Him gave evidence that they believed in Him, were simply obeying a command given to all of God's creation.

Now, when I hear other believers get bothered because someone who clearly does not know the Lord is praising Him, I tell them, "Leave them alone. They're simply doing what all of creation has been commanded to do." They praise Him because of what they know about Him. However, only those who are His children can worship Him – because they *know Him*.

"Blessed be the God and Father of our Lord Jesus Christ, Who according to His abundant mercy has begotten us again to a living hope through the resurrection of Jesus Christ from the dead, to an inheritance incorruptible and undefiled and that does not fade away, reserved in heaven for you."

1 Peter 1:3-4

~ *Chapter Eleven* ~

But Who Do You Say He Is?

"He saith unto them, "But who do you say that I am?" Matthew 16:15

In Matthew 16, we read where Jesus asked His disciples, "Who do men say that I, the Son of man am?" All the disciples answered, giving Him different answers for who men said that He was. Then our Lord asked them, "But Who do you say that I am?" Simon Peter answered Him, "You are the Christ, the Son of the living God." Jesus commended him for his answer – an answer that only the Father in heaven could have revealed to Peter.

The question, "Who do men say He is," was posed to you in the previous chapter. Now, I ask you, "But who do *you* say He is?" You have heard all that others have said about Him, but Who do *you* personally know Him to be?

From Chapter 1 of this book through Chapter 6, we learned that God is a God who brings comfort in our mourning (over sin and otherwise). We learned that His joy is the strength (the power) that will keep us out of the pit of despair and hopelessness that grief and guilt over our sins can present. We learned that He is our Abode – that no matter the church house that He plants us in (calls us to), or that we plant ourselves in, that we must ultimately be planted in Him. We learned that during times of offense that rather than backsliding and blacklisting Him that we should run *to* Him instead. We learned that His Word may very well offend (wound, sting) us, but that He will not leave us open and bleeding. We learned that offense can happen to us, no matter our position or maturity level, if our guards are down due to trials and circumstances. Lastly, we learned that we can even be offended by Christ and how He does, or does not do things. With all of that said, I ask you again, "But Who do *you* say He is?"

I will tell you who He is not. He is not sitting in heaven looking down on us, just waiting for us to sin so that He can pounce on us and punish us – or so that He can send down the lightning. We are told several times in the Holy Bible that God is slow to anger.[42] Many see the Lord as Punisher only, but that is due to living their lives according to the Law and not by grace. It is because they are religious and not relational when it comes to the living God. Take Job for instance. If you have never read all forty-two chapters of the Book, I encourage you to do so. Although Job never cursed God for what he was going through, there was a time that Job attributed what he was going through to God. He attributed it to the God of the Law and God the Judge. After all, God was the One who had authored and spoken the very Law that Job lived by and kept,[43] and God was the One Whom Job feared (was morally afraid of and reverent toward).[44] Although Job feared God, how well did he know God? Let's see.

In Chapter 42 of Job, we read these words from him, after complaining of God and justifying himself: "I know that You can do everything, And that no purpose of Yours can be withheld from You. You asked, 'Who is this who hides counsel without knowledge?' Therefore I have uttered what I did not understand, Things too wonderful for me, which I did not know. Listen, please, and let me speak; You said, 'I will question you, and you shall answer Me.' "I have heard of You by the hearing of the ear, But now my eye sees You. Therefore I abhor myself, And repent in dust and ashes." Job 42:2-6. After being personally enlightened (by way of his trials) to *Who* God is, what Job had just confessed to the Lord was his own ignorance of Him. Job confessed that he had only known of his God through others; through second-hand information; hearsay; *rumors*. He had not gotten to know Him for himself, not until his trials. Who is He rumored to be to you?

Just as it hurt Job physically, mentally, relationally (with his wife and his friends), and emotionally to suffer and to endure all that he did, we see in Job, Chapter 42 that God was not allowing Satan to do all that he did in order that Job would be harmed. Nor was it allowed as punishment. God allowed it because He knew the thoughts that He had toward Job – 'plans to prosper him [to mature him soulically]; not to harm him.'[45] (Words in brackets mine) Many times we go through, but unlike Job, we do curse God and die – fall away from Him altogether. Why is that? It is usually because we do not know God for ourselves. We have heard what others have had to say about Him. We know of Him through hearsay and rumors, rather than firsthand knowledge of Him through the disciplines of prayer and reading and studying His Word. Instead of knowing Him as the God of grace, most only know Him as God of the Law. *Knowing* Him is what helps going through trials and tests a little easier, and we won't automatically assume that what is happening is happening due to sin(s) in our lives, nor will anyone else be able to convince us of it if that is not truly the case.

If Christ was to ask His disciples today, as He did His disciples in Matthew 16, "Who do men say that I am," what would be your answer? Would you tell Him Whom He is rumored to be – what the preachers say, what your grandma or grandpa say, what your parents say, or even what your prayer partner says? There is no wrong answer, because the question was, "Who do men say that I am?" What if He then turns around and asks you, "But whom do you say that I am?" There is only one right answer, and that is the answer that is in line with what the Father has already said about His Son. Probably not all professed disciples today could answer that question. Notice again that Peter was the only one who answered. At his answer, Christ told him that no one could have revealed that to him except the Father.

In answer to Christ's question, only Peter answered Him. Maybe it was because Peter gave an answer before any of the other disciples could that we only see that he answered. What would cause me to not think that is that Jesus told him he could only know the answer he gave because the Fatherhad revealed it to him. Just as there are many who profess and do not follow, there are also many who profess but do not have a relationship with the Father. Why? In order to have a relationship with the Father, one must first believe in His Son as Who God says He is. Many do not.

In John 6:44a, Jesus says, "No one can come to Me, unless the Father Who sent Me draws him..." The only way that Christ will be revealed as Lord and all that He is to any man, woman, or child is if the Father Himself reveals it to him/her. Once the Father reveals it, we must then believe and not doubt. Has He revealed His Son to you?

Questions

1. Who is God to you?

2. In just one word, describe Him. *(You probably can't think of just one word.)*

3. What is your current perspective, or view, of God/Jesus?

4. When it comes to God, are you religious or relational?

5. How do you know?

6. At this stage in your walk with Christ, do you know Him more by secondhand information or firsthand experience?

7. Who do you say He is?

For all:

"Jesus is Lord!"

Ref. Romans 10:9

My Story

What I have learned is that believers' responses, or reactions, to trials show what we believe, in the moment. When trials present, our responses will show whether we believe that Jesus is Who God says He is. Our reactions will either show that we don't know Who He is, or that we have lost focus. My pastor has often said, "What we don't know is always more than what we do know; but, it's never more than *Who* we know." Trials come to try our faith. They also come to strengthen us and give us greater knowledge of Who God is.

Several years ago, the Lord spoke to me at a time when there wasn't even a hint of a trial. He told me that 'we (my family) would make it to the other side,' kind of like when He told the early disciples, "Come, let us go to the other side." Just like He didn't tell them that there would be a storm on the way, He also didn't tell me that there would be a storm.

Like Peter, there was a moment that I took my eyes off Christ, focused on the storm, and began to sink. Then, there were times that I asked, "Lord, don't You care?" Our Father was always there reminding me of Who He says His Son is, and encouraging me to keep agreeing with Him and to keep the faith.

"Beloved, do not think it strange concerning the fiery trial which is to try you, as though some strange thing happened to you; but rejoice to the extent that you partake of Christ's sufferings, that when His glory is revealed, you may also be glad with exceeding joy."

1 Peter 4:12-13

~ Chapter Twelve ~

You Too, Peter

"Now when the Sabbath was past, Mary Magdalene, Mary the mother of James, and Salome bought spices, that they might come and anoint Him. Very early in the morning, on the first day of the week, they came to the tomb when the sun had risen. And they said among themselves, "Who will roll away the stone from the door of the tomb for us?" But when they looked up, they saw that the stone had been rolled away–for it was large. And entering the tomb, they saw a young man clothed in a long white robe sitting on the right side; and they were alarmed. But he said to them, "Do not be

alarmed. You seek Jesus of Nazareth, Who was crucified. He is risen! He is not here. See the place where they laid Him. But go, tell His disciples—and Peter—that He is going before you into Galilee; there you will see Him, as He said to you." Mark 16:1-7

In Mark 14, we read where Jesus prophesied to His disciples that one of them would betray Him (v.18), that they would all be offended because of Him, would all forsake Him (v.27), and that Peter would deny Him (v.30). It is also in this same chapter that we read of Jesus' arrest and of His prophesies coming to pass. Judas betrayed Him to the chief priests and the scribes. Peter denied Him not once but three times, and before the cock crowed twice – just as our Lord had said. The other disciples forsook Him – deserted Him – just as our Lord had said. Why did they do it? Why did those who had followed Him so closely bail out on Him at a most crucial time in His life? I will tell you why. It was because they were offended by Him. There that word *offense* is again.

The Greek word for offense in this passage of Scripture is the same one that we discussed in a previous chapter of this book. It is skandalizō, which again means "to entrap, to trip up, to stumble, to fall away".[46] When Jesus' disciples saw Him being seized for arrest, they were most likely overcome with fear and a great desire to preserve their own lives. We can only imagine what was going on in their minds. They were probably tripping over the scene that was before them and stumbling over the idea that Jesus might really not be *Who* He said He was. Along with possibly questioning His identity, like John, they were probably taking a quick account of whether or not He was worth losing their lives for. So, because they were offended, they forsook Him. They fell away from Him because of offense. As they had so often done before, in faithless action, they were now questioning His identity – *again*.

Let us quickly look at Judas Iscariot and his betrayal of our Lord. Why did he do it? *Offense.*

Remember, as they sat around the table and ate, Jesus told all twelve of the disciples (to include Judas) that they would all be offended by Him and that one of them would betray Him that very night. However, He told them these things after the account of the woman who anointed Him with the contents of the alabaster box, in Mark 14, and also *after* Judas had already gone to the chief priests and the scribes to betray Him to them. Upon witnessing the woman breaking the box, which was considered to be very precious, the text tells us that some of the disciples became indignant, saying, "Why was this waste of the ointment made? For it might have been sold for more than three hundred pence, and have been given to the poor." At their indignant grumblings and murmurings, our Lord rebuked them. It is believed by some that the disciple who was the most indignant was Judas, because he was the disciple who was responsible for keeping the money. All of that – the indignant grumblings and Jesus' rebuke – happened in verses 6-9. In verse 10, we read that Judas went to the chief priests to betray Jesus. Judas betrayed Jesus because he was offended by His response to their indignant grumblings.

Now, let us look at Peter. Peter was passionate about our Lord, and we see that in many different accounts in the gospels of Matthew, Mark, Luke, and John.[47] Peter was the one who declared to our Lord that he would follow Him even to death.[48] He also refuted Jesus' prophesy that He would die, and Jesus rebuked him, telling him that he was only concerned with worldly cares.[49] It was this same Peter to whom the Father had revealed His Son's identity. It was also this same Peter who, upon hearing from our Lord that all of the disciples would desert Him, basically answered in no uncertain terms, "Maybe *they* will, but *I* won't." Jesus then told him in no uncertain terms, "Oh, you will be offended, Peter. So much so that you will deny (disown) Me three times before the cock crows twice."[50]

We later read that whenever the chief priests, scribes, and elders from the Jewish Sanhedrin arrived to arrest Jesus that Peter (in an effort to protect our

Lord and to possibly even thwart the arrest) cut off the ear of one of the soldiers.[51] There was no doubt that Peter loved his Lord, but if we will look closely at the aforementioned verses, we will come to another conclusion about Peter. He was reactionary. He was driven by his emotions. Peter seemed to say and do things out of emotional impulses, rather than thinking things through beforehand. Just as he, out of great emotion and passion for our Lord, declared his devotion to Him and how he would follow Him even unto death, he through emotion denied Him. He was no different than a lot of this current generation of disciples, was he? Emotions have their place. God gave us emotions, but He does not intend for us to be **driven** by them – *even concerning Him* – because emotions can cause us to make vows to Him that we either cannot, or will not be willing to, keep later on.

Then there are the other ten disciples, besides Peter – ten because Judas had already gone his own way. It was the other ten disciples who ran for their lives at Jesus' seizure. As the Lord had said, they were offended by Him; and because of it, they fell away from Him at the mere thought that He might not actually be Who He said He was and that Hemight really not be worth losing their lives for. They too were no different than a lot of us disciples today, were they?

You might be reading this and saying, "But I've never denied Christ, and I've never forsaken Him. I've been walking with Him all my life." You might truly be an exception to the rule, but let me ask you a couple of questions anyway. Have you ever sinned – *and that after becoming a Christian?* If the answer is, "Yes," then you have denied Him. Have you ever gone your own way or done your own thing, due to peer and societal pressures? Have you ever had an opportunity to tell someone about Him, but did not because you were afraid of what they would think about you or that you would be rejected by them? If the answer is, "Yes," then you have forsaken Him at some point. Peter denied Christ because He was ashamed of Him. The good news is this: Jesus was not shocked or caught off guard by His disciples' actions. He had already prophesied to

them His betrayal, His denial, and His desertion –
all by them. Judas, so remorseful over what he had
done, forfeited the handful of change that he sold
our Lord out for and later killed himself.[52] Peter,
the text tells us, wept after denying our Lord thrice
and upon immediately recalling Jesus' words that
he would deny Him.[53] Peter did not just cry softly
to himself either. The Greek word for wept in this
text is klaiō (pronounced *klah'-yo*) which means
"to sob; to wail aloud."[54] Again, Peter was no
doubt passionate about His Lord.

Nothing else is said about the other disciples in
this passage. We are just told that "they all forsook
Him, and fled." But imagine. Whenever we are
told that, 'He was wounded for our transgressions,
bruised for our iniquities, and that the chastisement
for our peace was upon Him; and by His stripes
we are healed,'[55] it must have been comforting for
the ten who deserted Him, and Peter, to know that
they were included in the *we*. Christ took the
desertion and the denial to the cross with Him –
and on that cross, He bore all sins to include theirs.
It was also on that cross that He prayed and

interceded for all, "Father, forgive them for they know not what they do."[56]

Christ knew that His disciples would be offended by Him. He told them that they would be. He also, after telling them that they would and that they would also forsake Him and that Peter would deny Him, told them that they would meet Him in Galilee after His resurrection.[57] It sounds to me like Jesus wanted them to not remain in the pit of despair, guilt, and grief that would result from their predicted sins. "Blessed are those who mourn, for they shall be comforted."[58] "Do not be sorry; for the joy of the Lord is your strength."[59] Christ brought comfort and hope to them before they fell short, and even after, with this message to the disciples, including Peter, 'Meet Me in Galilee,' for there is still yet work for you to do; and greater works they went on to do. Some of the disciples penned the gospels and other New Testament Books in the Bible (like James; I, II, and III John; and Acts). Peter preached the powerful sermon at Pentecost.[60] He went on to write I and II Peter, and signs and wonders followed him – so much so that people were healed just at the casting of his shadow.[61]

Not to diminish the roles and importance of the other disciples, because they all went on to do greater works in the name of the Lord. Peter stands out a little more though. Although all the disciples – on the heels of Peter's words – said that they would not deny the Lord, Peter represents those disciples in the forefront (present and future leaders). He represents those, like himself, who have on more than one occasion made public declarations to and about our Lord but fell away from Him due to offense. As a result of offense (either by others or by the conviction of the Word), they have denied Him – not once, but many times over. Like Peter, in their passion they pledged their devotion to Him, even that they would follow Him to death. Just as quickly and as passionately as they uttered those words, they just as quickly and as passionately denied Him through their words and their actions.

I have witnessed many great and potentially great leaders deny Christ. They got caught up in people, money, things, and/or bad and immoral habits – a cycle of denials. They denied Christ through their sinful actions and attitudes and their lifestyles, but then they also denied having denied Him. Unlike Peter, they would not own up to their sins. So, they remained in stagnation and denial – ministering but marching in marked time; not regressing, not progressing, just...*there*. But, Peter. When Peter became convinced of His sins, upon recalling the Lord's words to him, he was cut to the quick; and he wept – **LOUDLY**. There was no saving face for him.

2 Corinthians 7:9-10 says this: "Now I rejoice, not that you were made sorry, but that your sorrow led to repentance. For you were made sorry in a godly manner, that you might suffer loss from us in nothing. For godly sorrow produces repentance leading to salvation, not to be regretted; but the sorrow of the world produces death." What Paul was saying here is that he was not glad that the

people were made sorry, but because their sorrow brought about a change of heart and mind regarding their sins. He went on to tell them that they were made sorry in a godly manner – gently and lovingly, and not cut open and then left to bleed to death. Paul also told them that godly sorrow (sorrow that stems from knowing that you have sinned against God) produces deliverance not to be regretted. Worldly sorrow (sorrow that only stems from having been caught and/or after suffering loss because of the sin(s) produces death and no change of heart or mind. Repentance is not just saying, "God, I'm sorry," later to commit the same sin again. Repentance is not a 360° turn, but a 180° turn. Peter did a complete 180 regarding his sin. He bewailed his failure, and he did so loudly – not caring who saw or heard. Peter's mourning was indication of his conviction as well as his taking onus of his sin.

Imagine the comfort that must have come to Peter upon hearing the message from the Lord through the two Mary's and Salome – the message that Christ still wanted His disciples – *and, yes,*

Peter too – to meet Him in Galilee.[62] Peter's denial of the Lord was no greater a sin than the other disciples' desertion of Him. To Peter – sensitive, reactionary, and emotional Peter – it was probably grandiose. Peter's sin probably seemed bigger to him, because in making his declarations and in speaking his endearments to the Lord, his was not always an audience of One but of many. At least two or three of the other disciples were usually present.

But to have his mourning interrupted and cut off with the oh-so comforting message that Christ still desired His disciples *and him* to meet Him in Galilee... Again, Christ had already told the disciples before the desertion and the denials that they would meet Him in Galilee after His resurrection. We tend to either forget things in our times of mourning, or we just write ourselves out of the promise because we sinned. So, for Peter to hear those words – it must have been quite encouraging. Thank God for 'His mercies that are new every morning.'[63]

Through two little, but very profound words,

"…and Peter," Christ was letting Peter know thatthere was still work to be done in the future. He was letting Peter know that he was forgiven. He was letting him know that his sins did not define him nor did they discount him for ministry. He was letting Peter know that he was now to go on and strengthen the brethren. He was letting Peter know that there were still fish to be caught (souls to be won). He was letting Peter know that there were greater works to be done by him too. And Peter went on to do all that was entrusted of him – and with possibly a greater passion, because Jesus trusted him.

Many might look at the fact that Peter denied Christ three times and say that Peter's faith failed. I would dare propose to you that the real testing of Peter's faith did not come at the temptation to deny him, or even at the point of his denials. The real testing of his faith came when he answered the call to meet Christ in Galilee – to come out of his pit of misery and mourning, and to meet his Lord in the future.

I don't know which category you fall i nto –

disciple (layperson; disciple in the background) or Peter (leader; disciple in forefront) – but Christ has a message for you. If you have deserted Him, or if you have denied Him, and you now find yourself in a pit of misery and mourning, His message to you is, "Come out." He has risen; so, rise with Him. Come up out of your pit of misery, mourning, and despair, and meet Him in Galilee – your future. There are still works for you to do – Him through you. There are still brethren to strengthen.

Christ is saying to you, "Blessed are those who mourn, for they shall be comforted."[64] and, "...do not be sorry, for the joy of the Lord is your strength."[65] Acknowledge and confess your sin(s) to God, and do not remain in your sorrow. He is sending comfort to you at such a time as this to end your mourning. "Rejoice in the Lord always. Again, I will say, rejoice!"[66]

Hallelujah! The Lord is faithful, trustworthy, and unchanging! The meeting is still on!

Questions

1. For this book, Peter has been distinguished from the rest of Christ's disciples as a leader, or disciple in the forefront. What is your position? Are you a church leader?

2. Have you ever been offended by (ashamed of) our Lord?

3. Have you ever denied being associated with Jesus or deserted Him because of it?

4. All or most denials and desertions of Christ are rooted in offense. What's your story?

5. Have you received His restoration?

6. What was your restoration experience like?

7. Have you ever been deserted?

For you, Peter:

"God is not a man that He should lie; neither the son of man, that He should repent: hath He said, and shall He not do it..." Numbers 23:19

My Story

My oldest sister got saved when she was a teenager; and she was (and still is) on fire for the Lord. She has never been ashamed of the gospel and seized every opportunity to preach it to others – me included. Most often, my answer to her would be that I was going to wait to get saved, when I knew that I would not backslide. I wanted to be all in. I was young, and I had already seen so many other professed Christians backslide. I did not want to be one of them.

You see, I had a distorted picture of what being saved and filled with the Holy Spirit looks like. I had enough sense to know that I did not want to live a life that mocked God or one that would cause others to blaspheme Him. However, I did not have enough sense to know that how I live for Jesus – righteously or riotously – depends on how much I deny my flesh and subject it to the Holy Spirit's leading. It depends on whether I die to my flesh and all its lusts and desires and desire what He desires. It depends on whether I allow Christ – no longer *I* – to live in me.

I had my *You Too, Peter* moment, almost thirty years ago. I find that every offense that comes are opportunities to either remain faithful to Him or to deny Him. My choice.

"Who Himself bore our sins in His own body on the tree, that we, having died to sins, might live for righteousness—by Whose stripes you were healed. For you were like sheep going astray, but have now returned to the Shepherd and Overseer of your souls."

1 Peter 2:24-25

Outro

For years, I have known that I was supposed to write books, and that the gifting and the grace to do so come from God. At times, I did wonder, "When, Lord?" It was like being pregnant with a baby, and only knowing that you are pregnant but having no due date. Yet, you are assured that the baby would come forth. Early in September of 2009, on a Sunday afternoon, my family had returned home from a church service; and after I saw that our children were taken care of and that they and Pastor Randy were had lunch, the Holy Spirit led me to the loft in my home. He said nothing, but with what seemed like fluid motion, I got Bible, pen, and brand-new notebook and went upstairs. Once there, within a matter of just a few hours (three to four), the first three chapters of *A Message for the Disciples...You Too, Peter* were written. The baby's head had crowned! The last push came on October 9, 2009, and what you have just read is the result of what God has formed...*just for you.*

Even after giving birth to four children, the wonderment and the amazement of just how awesome and all-knowing God is never diminished. Instead, it grew with the birth of each child. As I held each newborn baby in my arms, I marveled at the majesty of God and how each toe, finger, and everything else was in just the right places. I also beheld the hair and the fingernails, wondering just where He got the ingredients to make them. "Was that in me," I would ask myself in astonishment. The conclusion that I came to is that neither my husband nor I had absolutely anything to do with the *forming* of those babies. Yes, he housed the seed, and I housed the egg and the womb – but *God,* and only God could have divinely provided it all and is responsible for the formation of each of them. To say the least, that is how I see this book. As I read each of the chapters after they were written, I marveled at my God, the Father, and the Creator of all, and how I was yet again only a vessel to house and to now bring forth another of His works – this message for Christ's disciples – *and Peter.* Just like my natural children, this book also has purpose.

When I began writing it, I had no idea what the overall message was – just that it was a message from God to His people. Around about Chapter 7, I knew though. God is dealing with and confronting offense, and He desires to heal the souls of His people. The healing might hurt even more than the initial wounding, but I pray that you will allow Him do what He desires to do. This book may only be a beginning, or you may have read it just at the cusp of your manifested healing. Just know that our Lord will not leave you open and bleeding.

Several years ago, I accidentally cut one of my my thumbs – with a butter knife of all things. The cut was very deep, and the bleeding was so profuse that it resulted in a trip to the Emergency Room. Because there were so many other patients to be seen, and having more "dire issues than a cut thumb" (according to the attending physician), the cut was cleaned and glued rather than stitched. Before I was discharged, the doctor warned me that the cut might get infected; which was a common result of gluing versus stitching.

A few days later, due to the wound oozing pus and a swollen thumb, I suspected that it might be infected. So, I made yet another trip to the hospital – only that time it was to the Family Medicine Clinic, with hopes of being seen as a walk-in patient. After waiting a short time, with my then three- and six-year-old sons, a nurse called me back to an examination room. At first glance, she confirmed my suspicions. The wound was infected; so, she proceeded to remove the glue. That part was not bad at all, but then... Then she began to squeeze the wound. She told me that the infection was deep down in the tissue; therefore, it had to be squeezed in order to get it out and to prevent it from getting further into my bloodstream. She also warned that the squeezing would probably hurt worse than the initial cut; and she squeezed, and squeezed it. It did hurt more than it had when I had first cut it! It was very painful, and at first I was trying to save face for my two young children that were with me; but then verbally (with no cussing or swearing) and facially, I had to admit that the squeezing hurt – *BAD*. After she was done squeezing the wound, the nurse washed it. Since the exam room that I was in was not a regular exam room, the bed that I was seated on was steel. As the nurse squeezed and washed the wound, I held on to the bed with my good hand; and I promise you, I felt as though I was strong enough to bend that metal. Many times, we do not realize just how much offense can actually be used to strengthen us until it is being worked out of us.

Before leaving the clinic that day, the nurse advised me to keep the wound uncovered. She said that way it could air out. After seeing her, I saw a doctor, who prescribed an antibiotic to get rid of any infection that might have still been lingering.

On my way out of the clinic, I ran into the attending nurse, who strongly advised me, "Make sure that you take all of the medicine, even though you will notice a difference by tonight. Also, make sure that you take it at the prescribed times." I did. The wound healed so nicely that today I have to look really hard to see the scar that was left. That is what God desires to do with our souls. He desires to heal us so nicely that others would have to look really hard to see the scars – even when we point them out to them by way of testimonies. But in order to have God do anything about the wounds, we have to air them out. We must be honest with Him and tell Him that we are wounded (offended) and when we have wounded (offended) Him and others. He may also lead us to confess it to someone else who is mature enough to pray with us and not judge us or gossip. Squeezing and a deep washing will come, but they are for getting the infection (bitterness, anger, resentment, and unforgiveness, to name a few) out. They will most likely come by way of God-ordained or God-permitted circumstances as well as by way of His Word, which as we have read will offend or will most likely cause even more pain. Just as it will offend, His Word will also serve as the Antibiotic, which we will have to take at prescribed times – daily and nightly (ref. Joshua 1:8) in order to kill any remaining infection; because if it is not killed, it will most assuredly infect the rest of the Body.

Whoever you are – lay-member or leader – if you bought this book or were given it, it is because the messages that it contains from the heart of the Father is intended for your heart. In the midst of your mourning, He wants to get a message to you. Will you receive it? Will you heed the command to meet Him where He is – in Galilee – in your future? As I, by living many of the messages, have been strengthened through it, I pray that you have also.

His,

Juanita

"And in those days Peter stood up in the midst of the disciples (altogether the number of names was about a hundred and twenty), and said, "Men and brethren, this Scripture had to be fulfilled..."

Acts 1:15-16a

About the Author

Juanita is a native of Clemson, South Carolina, and an Air Force veteran. She is married to Randy, who is also an Air Force veteran. They have four sons. The Davises have lived in Goldsboro, North Carolina; Okinawa, Japan; and North Las Vegas, Nevada. They currently reside in Randy's hometown of Galesburg, Illinois, where Randy is the Pastor of Community Temple Church of God in Christ.

Juanita has written three books (including this revision) and has contributed to two women's devotional collaborations. For more information about her books, visit her website at **www.juanitaedavis.com**.

References

Introduction

1. James Strong, *The New Strong's Expanded Dictionary of Bible Words* (Nashville: Thomas Nelson Publishers, 2001). Also available in CD ROM.

Chapter One

2. James Strong, *The New Strong's Expanded Dictionary of Bible Words* (Nashville: Thomas Nelson Publishers, 2001). Also available in CD ROM.

3. 1 Corinthians 13:12 and James 1:23

4. 1 John 1:9

Chapter Two

5. James Strong, *The New Strong's Expanded Dictionary of Bible Words* (Nashville: Thomas Nelson Publishers, 2001). Also available in CD ROM.

6. James Strong, *The New Strong's Expanded Dictionary of Bible Words* (Nashville: Thomas Nelson Publishers, 2001). Also available in CD ROM.

7. Hebrews 13:8

8. Hebrews 4:15

9. Hebrews 4:15

10. Hebrews 4:16

11. 2 Corinthians 2:15

Chapter Three

12. Galatians 5:22-23b

13. John 17:21

14. Psalm 34:8

Chapter Four

15. Job 23:2, 10-12

16. Psalm 37:23

17. 1 Peter 4:8

18. Luke 23:34a

19. James Strong, *The New Strong's Expanded Dictionary of Bible Words* (Nashville: Thomas Nelson Publishers, 2001). Also available in CD ROM.

20. The King James version

21. Psalm 119:34 (reference)

Chapter Five

22. James Strong, *The New Strong's Expanded Dictionary of Bible Words* (Nashville: Thomas Nelson Publishers, 2001). Also available in CD ROM.

23. James Strong, *The New Strong's Expanded Dictionary of Bible Words* (Nashville: Thomas Nelson Publishers, 2001). Also available in CD ROM.

24. John Gill, *John Gill's Exposition of the Entire Bible.* http:// www.e-sword.net/commentaries.html. CD Rom.

25. 1 Timothy 2:5

26. Hebrews 13:5b

27. Isaiah 34:3 and Matthew 12:20

28. Matthew 5:4

29. Hebrews 12:6a

Chapter Six

30. Matthew 3:1 and 3:3b

31. Matthew 3:13-14

32. Luke 1:41-44

33. James Strong, *The New Strong's Expanded Dictionary of Bible Words* (Nashville: Thomas Nelson Publishers, 2001). Also available in CD ROM.

34. Psalm 46:10

Chapter Eight

35. Judges 17:16 and 21:25

36. *Merriam-Webster's Dictionary* (Merrim-Webster's, Incorporated, 2001). CD ROM version.

37. James Strong, *The New Strong's Expanded Dictionary of Bible Words* (Nashville: Thomas Nelson Publishers, 2001). Also available in CD ROM.

38. John 10:10

Chapter Nine

39. John 9:7

Chapter Ten

40. *Merriam-Webster's Dictionary* (Merriam-Webster's, Incorporated, 2001). CD ROM version.

41. John 14:6

Chapter Eleven

42. Nehemiah 9:17; Psalm 103:8, 145:8; Joel 2:13; Jonah 4:2; Nahum 1:3

43. Job 1:1

44. *Merriam-Webster's Dictionary* (Merriam-Webster's, Incorporated, 2001). CD ROM version.

45. Jeremiah 29:11

Chapter Twelve

46. James Strong, *The New Strong's Expanded Dictionary of Bible Words* (Nashville: Thomas Nelson Publishers, 2001). Also available in CD ROM.

47. Matthew 14-26; Mark 8-14; Luke 5-24 and John 6-21

48. Matthew 26:35 and Luke 22:33

49. Matthew 16:23; Mark 8:33 and Luke 4:8

50. Matthew 26:34-35, 75 and Mark 14:30-31, 72

51. Matthew 26:51; Mark 14:47; Luke 22:50 and John 18:10

52. Matthew 27:3-5 and Acts 1:15-19

53. Matthew 26:75; Mark 14:72 and Luke 22:62

54. James Strong, *The New Strong's Expanded Dictionary of Bible Words* (Nashville: Thomas Nelson Publishers, 2001). Also available in CD ROM.

55. Isaiah 53:5

56. Luke 23:34

57. Matthew 26:32 and Mark 14:28

58. Matthew 5:4

59. Nehemiah 8:10

60. Acts 2:14-42

61. Acts 5:15

62. Matthew 26:32 and Mark 14:28

63. Lamentations 3:22-23

64. Matthew 5:4

65. Nehemiah 8:10

66. Philippians 4:4

One last thought...

"Sticks and stones may break my bones, but words will never hurt," is a lie. Words can and do hurt, even if we are carrying hurtful words to someone that someone else has said about them. In the few times that I have been on the receiving end – with the carrier being someone that I thought cared about me – I have thought, and at times asked (while reeling from the sting of the words), "Why would you tell me that? Did you tell me to hurt me? And, what did *you* say to defend me?" Being our brother's keeper requires that we not take the knife from his back and then stab him in the heart.

Made in the USA
Monee, IL
02 December 2024

70564195R00115